KIDS, DOGS, CANARIES, AND OTHER CURIOSITIES

HAL REICHARDT

For
Shannon, Lindsay, and Conor

Contents

Police Line Do Not Cross

The police normally try to steer clear of my children's bathroom, and with good reason, but I had to call them in last week when the toilet clogged up. I needed some of that yellow tape that they use to cordon off a crime scene. I know the government has already expanded its investigations beyond all reason, but there was no getting around this new evidence of a vast right-wing conspiracy after I pulled a second diaper from the glossy knoll.

It all started innocently enough with a plea from my family to fix the toilet for the fourth time this month. Like a good dad, I slung the plunger around my back, loaded up on air fresheners, and announced that I was going in.

There followed a brutal battle between man and bowl that I don't care to recount in great detail. Suffice to say that tidal waves are not confined to the world's great oceans, as previously thought. And men, be careful with the new brand of plunger that promises to be five times more powerful than a blast from an elephant. I could have told the people in marketing that elephants and toilets don't mix, but exaggeration has become something of a standard, and I suppose there's no use wasting a stamp on that complaint.

I soon realized that even an elephant plunger was not going to get to the bottom of this one. It was time for the real tools. Time to unhook the water supply, bail out the bowl, and yank the whole thing from its moorings, wax seal and all.

After casing the toilet for a few minutes I turned off the water supply (righty tighty!). That was a good start. But you can't very well get the toilet off the floor without disconnecting the water line from the toilet tank. If you are guessing lefty loosey at this juncture, you are mistaken.

Once upon a time, a nut was a nut. You could put a crescent wrench on one, turn to the left, add some mystery oil if necessary, and disassemble just about anything ever built. But that was too simple. Today, I've got a nut on the water supply to my toilet that will spin to the left with ease, but just won't come off no matter how much I plead. It won't go back on either. I got the nut halfway to nowhere and couldn't get back.

At this point, my testosterone level was getting dangerously low, so I got a bigger wrench and went at the water line from the other end. This part was plastic, so I had every reason to smell success. The plastic was squared off, so the wrench went on real snug. Obviously, this was the place to unhook the water supply.

It took a bit of muscle, but I soon was able to break a large piece of plastic off the tank. I watched in dismay as the plastic slid down the pipe to join up with the nut that got nowhere.

With nothing left to fix on the outside of the toilet, I decided to put the tools away and just make like none of this ever happened. My family was out, so a cover-up could be accomplished with relative ease.

I turned the water supply back on just long enough to confirm that I am not and never will be a plumber. Water streamed out of both ends of the line while the dumb nut and the broken plastic just sat there in the middle like nothing was wrong.

That's when I called the cops. The children pleaded with me not to make a Federal case out of this, but they are not up on the latest issues of importance to average citizens that are being worked on in the nation's capitol. And they didn't mind the police tape that kept them from getting to the crime scene because it gave them clear title to clog up the other bathroom while the plumber was in there gathering evidence with the FBI.

When they got the toilet off the floor, I was able to pull out not one, but two diapers. That raised a few eyebrows! My kids now think I'm a hero for unclogging the toilet, and the FBI was so happy to find the first hard evidence of corruption in high places that they gave me a tape recorder just for fun. They took the diapers down to forensics for detailed analysis, but I know what they're going to find. Politics is a dirty business.

Swing Low Sweet Chandelier

Miracles rarely start out as home improvement projects. You usually have to have someone from the Bible around, or at least a saint or two to make those impossible dreams come true. But we bucked the trend at our place just last week.

After twelve years in the same house, things start to leave formation. So I gathered the whole family around and announced that we were all going to embark on a fix-it campaign. I wanted everything in the house put back in line. Like the faucet in the downstairs bathroom that was missing a handle on one side for the last few years (ever since I installed it). And the vinyl floor in the laundry room where the dog dug a hole so that he could bury my checkbook. But most of all, the chandelier in the dining room that dropped down a few feet from the ceiling one day so that it could bonk people on the head when they walk by and stop you from playing miniature pool on Friday nights.

That chandelier did look good on the walk-through before we signed the papers to buy our house. Everything looked good that day. When we came in the front door, angels swept past us to the dining room and danced on that chandelier. It shone like a beacon in a brass ring. Light reflected off the facets in the glass and played on the freshly painted walls like an invitation to the heavenly host.

But after we signed the mortgage, the angels moved to another new house and left behind a one-thousand-pound lighting fixture in the middle of a ten-by-ten room. Before long, the chandelier dropped down halfway to the floor like Quasimodo ringing the bell in the Notre Dame, but without the music.

And that's where it stayed for the next ten years.

Getting it down off the ceiling wasn't too difficult. I just got out the stepladder, unscrewed a few bolts, and stuck my head underneath the thing to break its fall.

But now the question was, what to do with this chandelier. My first thought was to give it to charity, but when the guys in the pickup truck came around, they sailed right past it and made rude catcalls like they were standing up a blind date. So the chandelier sat in the corner of our garage for a week looking like a Cinderella with two missing shoes.

Then one day, my wife and I noticed one of those big dumpsters down the street in front of a neighbor's house. It had a sign on the side that said "Absolutely no Chandeliers," but that didn't stop us.

We waited until dark, and nonchalantly slipped down the sidewalk with the chandelier, like we were just out for a constitutional after supper and couldn't find the dog, so decided to rip the chandelier off the ceiling and walk that instead.

We got all the way to the edge of the dumpster, when some friendly neighbors pulled out of their driveway and shone their headlights on the two of us holding the chandelier. And for one magical moment it was like the angels returned. The chandelier lit up like a searchlight at a Hollywood premier so that the neighbors could take a few snapshots.

Seizing the initiative, I yelled out over the noise of the car engine to see if our neighbors could spare any of those candle kind of light bulbs that fit in chandeliers, and helped my wife hoist the whole thing up a bit higher so they could see we were sincere.

When word got around that we pulled a broken chandelier from the dumpster and fixed it with nothing but a few new light bulbs, our picture ended up in the community newspaper along with a story about our heroic recycling efforts. We don't mind the good publicity, but hold off on those donations, please. We've already got plenty of used chandeliers in the garage. And there are only so many angels to go around.

Donuts For Everyone

There are some people living at our house that I hardly know, and it's making me a little uneasy. I'm talking about the contractors. We've got three painters in the family room right now watching the morning show while the rest of the family gets ready to go to work or summer camp. There's plenty of coffee for everybody, but we're running short on frosted donuts.

Last night, there was a man outside my bedroom window right before bedtime. He wasn't trying to look in or anything, and the shade was drawn. But his ghostly silhouette flitting by the window every now and then unnerved me. I just can't watch sitcoms the right way when a man is hanging around my upstairs window.

Go home already! It's nine o'clock. Time for bed. But the dedication of contractors knows no limits. They may not come to work when you expect them to, but they do stay longer than most house guests.

After a while, I get tired of trying to find things for all these contractors to do. They need a lot of mental stimulation to stay on top of their games, and I'm not the best at playing Yahtze. So I invited in some more contractors over to keep the other guys company and brought home a few cases of Red Bull to keep everyone on the ball.

One thing I like about the contractors is their international know-how. All the siders are from Mexico and most of the painters come from Lithuania. The masons are from Texas, another foreign country. The contractors all speak the real languages, so it isn't easy to communicate with them. My Lithuanian has always been weak, so I use a lot of hand gestures when I'm trying to explain how to clean up the paint that got spilled on the deck out back. This usually results in a lot of smiles and nods of approval all around, so I think I may be getting through.

I like the schedules that contractors keep too (one for me and one for them). They don't seem to worry about this nine to five on Monday through Friday business. Instead, they breeze in when they are truly inspired. Only then do they get to work. If my house ends up looking like the Sistine Chapel when they're done, I won't be too surprised. These guys are that good.

There's another guy very similar to the Pope who only comes around in the mornings and gives the benediction to the whole crew in the driveway out front. He doesn't do any work himself, but everyone goes ooh and ah when he points to the house and raises his hands to the sky in a plea for divine intervention.

We need that kind of baptism with our house because it definitely needed to be born again. It suffered for years with only one jack-of-all-trades (me) tending to its needs, and was showing the strains of fidelity. But the contractors are fixing that.

They don't have attachment issues like I do. Have you got a codependency thing going with the defective siding that you had to paint five times in six years? Not anymore. Just rip it out with crowbars and throw it on the lawn. Not entertaining enough for you? Well, then let's just pull the ten-ton pickup truck with the monster tires sideways into the driveway and blast the salsa music on the stereo while everyone lollygags about sipping Red Bull for awhile. No dancing until Friday night.

Things are getting really crowded around the dinner table these days. And it's not easy to say grace in several different languages before you dig in. After I said a prayer in a mixture of Lithuanian and Spanish the other night, the contractors got mad and refused to eat dessert. Man, than hurts. I may never make another batch of homemade donuts, even though our dog Joey said they were great.

Dogs Who Love Too Much

"Get a dog," my father said, and for once I thought I could go along. Sure, a dog, I thought. I remember that from boyhood. A frisky ball of fur and teeth always happy to jump up on your clothes with muddy paws and sneak out the front door when you're not looking. A surfer dog of the suburbs, destined to ride the unbridled enthusiasm of dogness from one neighbor's lawn to the next, while its owner trails the action with an untethered leash held high overhead like a flag from a losing battle.

Yeah. That was fun. The kind of experience you want your own son to remember some day when he's older. It's for the children, you understand.

So we opened the door to our future, and in came Joey. We tried to name him Chandler, but my son decided he wasn't that kind of friend. He was more like Joey. He's a Golden Retriever, so I'm thinking he'll bring back the good times one of these days.

I thought I knew the animals. I knew the cat, the canary, and Chip the Chunk (our guinea pig). We understood each other in a basic sort of way. I put out the food, and they ate. We rarely made eye contact. But Joey wants to get involved in every little thing we do. When I hug my wife in the kitchen, I get the sad eyes from Joey that he's not feeling the love. But that doesn't stop him. He gets his nose right in your business with absolutely no shame. If we were all scratch and sniff cards from the lottery, Joey would have made us millionaires by now.

Rich dog, poor dog, Joey doesn't care. He likes to lick them all. And if you're not a dog, that's OK too. Joey will lick your hand, your pants, your face. Anything. Once he gets licking, there's no stopping him. He's a slobber monster.

When it comes to home furnishings, Joey is an impact player. The kind of guy you draft in the first round, who takes you to the promised land of the Super Bowl to claim your share of sports history. Too bad Joey got the Super Bowl confused with the toilet bowl. He made some kind of statement by emptying the entire bowl in one afternoon all by himself. And they say football is a team game.

He did better with the new carpet. Most people wouldn't have even noticed the threads popping out of the new carpet where it once met up with the hardwood floor. It was the kind of installation error that could easily be overlooked. But Joey saw a problem there, and got right to work unraveling the entire living room. This is a process known in the world of high technology as reverse engineering. And now that I see how carpet is really made, I'm not that impressed.

When it comes to dental care for all those canine teeth, Joey is a dog's dog. Instead of a silly little toothpick, Joey likes to tear a branch out of the hedge out back and gnaw that to smithereens. I keep finding little bits of bark and wood all over the house, as if I needed a Hansel and Gretel trail of crumbs to find my way to the back yard.

I'm glad we live in the great Northwest, because Joey likes all kinds of forest products. I sent a letter to the Forest Service offering Joey's help thinning out the dangerous underbrush in the Cascades, but I haven't heard back from them yet. Meanwhile, Joey eats napkins like people eat candy bars. When he swipes one off the kitchen table, he knows he's bad and runs like a beggar to his safe place on the green cushion. I named the cushion Green Acres in homage to an old TV show that Joey doesn't even know about. But he knows Green Acres is a neutral country like Switzerland, so that's where he goes when he's done something illegal, like eating a napkin in one gulp.

When Joey first came to us as a puppy, our friends thought we were crazy, because we had just finished remodeling our house. We had new carpet, paint, and furniture for almost a month before Joey made the scene. The house was almost perfect.

But Joey changed all that.

There's a theory about the universe called entropy, which says that order is unusual in the big scheme of things. That stuff is bound to fall apart over time. Joey loves entropy and works hard every day to remind us that the world is not a perfect place. He proves the futility of fussing to the last millimeter, knowing inches and yards are just waiting to overwhelm our small concerns.

But he's always happy to see us, and never stops loving us back, which is more than we can say for the new furniture.

Dog Journals

I always suspected our dog Joey was up to something, but it wasn't until I discovered his journals that the full scope of his ambitions was revealed. I was shocked when I discovered his notebook, because Joey never gives any indication of the kind of motor skills needed to write a decent memoir (unless it's also an audio book and that's what the barking is all about).

All I see are the same things day after day. He barks and runs around in the back yard when he's on an upper. Other times, he beats up the Beta dog in the family room and steals the napkins from the dinner table like they were wheat thins. The Beta dog was once a proud stuffed animal from a good department store, but has now been reduced to little more than a pelt. But let's take a sneak peek inside Joey's journals and hear his side of the story.

Monday. Woke up and looked around. I noticed someone behind me wagging his tail, and chased him around the house for a while. Couldn't catch the scoundrel, so I barked. Then the people came downstairs. When they turned on the porch light and looked out into the back yard, I stood at point with my ears pricked up for that cover-of-the-dog-food look. When we couldn't find the prowler, I gave them my best sad eyes look, and scored a beef jerky on the spot.

Tuesday. Wash day is the saddest day of the week. They take all the good snacks out of the hiding places and put them in huge piles. It's enough to get a dog excited. Then they stuff all the goodies into the white dudes in the corner room, and walk away while those guys choke and spit in disgust. Happens every week, so I've given up trying to stop that torture. I just hope they don't find the underwear that I stashed in the doghouse. I'm saving them for the movie later.

Wednesday. Out for a walk today, and I splashed in every puddle along the way. Nose first like a submarine into the big ones. Memo to marketing: let's name that new perfume Wet Dog.

Thursday. When night came, they closed the sliding glass door to the back yard. And there was that dumb dog in the window again looking right at me! He's got a lot of nerve coming right up to the window in my yard. But the more I bark, the more he barks back. Let me tell you, this dog is one scary bundle. But when the people lowered the blind, he disappeared. Chicken.

Friday. Shopping day. I pretended that I wouldn't eat my regular food again, so the mom would buy me some goodies at the store. She brought home some crackers last week, and got mad when I ate the bags before she was done unloading the car. So, I didn't help out this week. When in doubt, I go back to my cushion. That's the dog way.

Saturday. Something went wrong right away today. The man who usually disappears during the day stayed at the kitchen table and hogged all the cereal. So I pitched in with the chores to show my worth to the family. They have a noisy monster that they push around on the floor. It eats everything in its path, so I have to work fast to snarf the good crumbs before the monster gets to them. Then there's the drooler. I thought I was sloppy until I met this idiot. He can't bark at all, and just slides around on the floor getting everything wet. Then they punish him for making a mess by squeezing his face over the sink. Poor guy. I tried to help by covering his tracks, but that made the people even more upset.

Sunday. Out for a walk today. Stopped by my girlfriend's house and rubbed noses through the chain-link fence. She looked cute and wagged her tail. We have a jailhouse kind of thing going on. Visitations are strictly limited, and the guards watch our every move.

Joey's journals got a little repetitious after that. And he could be back any minute, so I'd better sign off. I don't want him to get any more suspicious. He already knows we're watching.

Licking For A Living

I don't worry about burglars breaking into our house because I know our dog Joey will probably lick them to death before they can get out of the foyer. He's a Golden Retriever with a big tongue that is hanging out all the time looking for something to work on. That something is usually me or my pants leg.

I think I'm just for practice, because he never gets excited when I come home from work. Somehow, I thought dogs were supposed to greet their keepers at the door when they come home from another day's hard work. But when I drag myself into the house, Joey lays there on the floor and hardly raises an eyebrow. It's almost like he's saying, "Oh, you again. Where have you been all day?"

I guess I shouldn't have watched so many episodes of *The Flintstones* when I was young. At the beginning of every program, while the theme song was running, Fred Flintstone's dog, Dino, would knock him down at the door to the house because he was so excited. I got conditioned to think that's how a dog should act. My dog Joey doesn't exactly look like a purple dinosaur, but I don't accept that for an excuse.

Just try explaining the concept of working for a living to a dog. That's right. They just don't get it, and why should they? If all you had to do was lay on the floor, wag your tail, and lick a few strangers to make a living, wouldn't you be blase too about the concept of work?

So I get no reaction when I come in the door. But when I sit down in front of the TV, now all of the sudden I'm Joey's best friend. He lifts my hand with his wet nose in a not-so-subtle reminder to pet him and scratch his ears. Then he licks the back of my hand to show how much he appreciates the attention. Too bad I don't like getting slobbered.

There's a boy down the street who plays with my son once in a while. He seems to be afraid of dogs. So I thought I'd use our dog Joey to help him get over his fear. But the boy would have none of it. I asked him why he didn't like dogs, expecting to hear something about big teeth and getting bit in the leg. But he said simply, "I don't like to get licked."

Now that made sense. End of conversation. And it's too bad, because dogs really can be man's best friends.

There must be something that needs to get licked in this world, and when I find it, I'm going to put Joey on the job. In the old days, you had to lick a stamp before you put it on an envelope, but now they come with some kind of space-age glue that you don't have to get wet. The kitchen floor needs a good mopping at least once a week. The problem there is that Joey's tongue leaves streaks, kind of like the opposite of Windex. Maybe if I gave him a shot of Windex in the morning for breakfast we could fix this problem. But dogs shouldn't be drinking on the job.

Licking can be good for cuts and scrapes. A dog's mouth is actually much cleaner than a normal person's mouth. I read that somewhere, but I just don't believe it. How could it be? Whoever said that probably never watched what a dog gets into in the back yard.

Dogs only have two ways to relate to the world, through their nose and mouth. So everything gets tested in there. This is not hygienic. So when I get a cut, I prefer to use some antibiotic cream and a band-aid. We'll let the person who said dogs have clean mouths test that hypothesis on his own cuts and scrapes.

Geez. We're running out of things for Joey to do! Seems like the only activities he's qualified for are eating, sleeping, walking, and licking anyone who comes to our front door. It's a small contribution, to be sure, but it keeps the people selling magazines and cookies happy.

Detective Dog

Detective Dog was whizzing down Route 26, his head stuck out the window and one paw on the wheel. His head was spinning like the tires on the asphalt.

He'd spent the last few weeks looking for Kissy Cat, whom he knew was hiding somewhere in the neighborhood. Someone had to stop that cat. Scotch tape had been disappearing for weeks from different houses in the neighborhood, and Christmas was only two weeks away.

Meanwhile, Kissy Cat had been spotted tooling around in her 1973 Cadillac, wearing a big pink bow in her hair, listening to Al Green CDs, with the back seat of her car overflowing with premium scotch tape.

Dog never set out to be a detective. It was more like detective work found him. And he had a nose for it. He was what the humans called a Golden Retriever. And so naturally, he got a lot of work finding missing people and other stuff and bringing them back. And there was no one in the neighborhood who could do it better than Detective Dog.

Kissy Cat was a long-hair, part Siamese with some other kind of breed mixed in. She was expelled from the Animal Orphanage for shredding all the wrapping paper right before the headmaster's birthday. After that, she wandered into Detective Dog's neck of the woods, trying to look innocent and looking for unsuspecting victims for her schemes.

Detective Dog pulled his 1958 Thunderbird into the parking lot at East Elementary School to set up a command post. He kept a watchful eye as the maintenance man whacked the weeds around the parking lot with a funny looking stick. Nothing suspicious about that, he thought.

Then Detective Dog spotted Johnny Lawful from the neighborhood on his way back to school after lunch recess. Johnny was the kind of kid you could count on to give you the straight scoop. Detective Dog had worked with him on a few cases before.

Johnny looked like most eleven-year-olds, but maybe a little cooler. His black hair was spiked up like you see in the Saturday-morning cartoons on TV. And he could talk to dogs like it was no problem. That's what made Johnny a valuable informant. He saw Detective Dog in the front seat of the car and came over to say hello.

"Johnny boy, how's it hanging?" said Detective Dog.

"All right, dog. I'm late for fourth period though. What's up?"

"I'm looking for Kissy Cat. There's been a lot of scotch tape missing around the neighborhood, and I've got a feeling Kissy Cat is really going to throw the holidays out of whack this time."

"That explains it," said Johnny. "My mom thought I used all the scotch tape and got mad at me. Now I know it was Kissy Cat all along."

"Listen Johnny," said Detective Dog. "I need your help on this one. Check with the other kids at school and see if there's been any missing scotch tape at anybody else's house. Christmas is only two weeks away."

"OK dog. I'll check it out," said Johnny. "See you after school."

26

Well, that was enough work for one morning, he thought. So Detective Dog took a nap in the front seat of his Thunderbird. Nice.

Meanwhile, two blocks over on River Drive, Kissy Cat was cruising around in her Cadillac. The back seat was still overflowing with scotch tape and Marvin Gaye was playing on the stereo. Ideas were swirling in her brain. Big ideas. Like what she was going to do with all that scotch tape. Kissy Cat figured the Army might just be interested in getting their hands on that scotch tape so that they could put Iraq back together after the war. And Kissy Cat wanted the contract. But she needed more proof to show the Army that she could deliver the massive quantities needed.

Kissy Cat wheeled her Cadillac into the parking lot of the 7-11 and got herself a Big Gulp. You have to think big when you're dealing with the Army, she thought. She rubbed her black fur on the trash can out front and waited for Deep Dan to call.

Deep Dan was all grown up, so Kissy Cat knew he couldn't be trusted. But she needed an in with the Defense Department, and Deep Dan knew the right people over there. People who needed scotch tape and weren't afraid to pay good money for it.

Suddenly, Kissy Cat's cell phone rang. She had it programmed to play a different Motown song whenever there was an incoming call. Anything to keep Detective Dog off her tail. It was Deep Dan on the line.

"Meet me in the parking lot of the 7-11 in ten minutes," said Deep.

Kissy Cat smiled at her good luck, thinking that this was going to be just her kind of caper.

Deep Dan arrived dressed in a brown suit that fit him like a shopping bag filled with oranges. He had a few wisps of hair laying limply on his nearly bald head, and he wore X-Ray Vision glasses that he thought nobody knew about.

But Kissy Cat knew about the glasses. Ever since she was thrown out the window of a seven-story apartment building just because she chewed through the Christmas tree lights, Kissy Cat knew people couldn't be trusted. She had to watch from the alley as her old owners got new lights and celebrated Christmas without her. From that moment on, Kissy Cat was determined to get even with the world.

Deep Dan pulled his brown Ford Fiesta into the parking lot and walked over to the side of the 7-11, where Kissy Cat was hanging out. Deep scanned the surroundings with his X-Ray Vision glasses and thought he saw something inside the dumpster. He jumped in head first and let out a few judo chops. Then he came back out of the dumpster. He shook his head and opened his briefcase. Inside was a nine-by-eleven glossy photo of Detective Dog asleep at the wheel of his Thunderbird in the elementary school parking lot.

"It's Detective Dog," said Deep. "He's onto us. And he's got that darn Johnny Lawful helping out. We're going to have to change our tactics or abort the mission."

"Gee," said Kissy Cat. "What good are those X-Ray Vision glasses if you're just going to get upset every time you see something?"

"My contacts at the agency are very interested in your little proposal," said Deep Dan. "We'll take all the scotch tape you can get your claws on, but it has to be the good kind. None of that dime-store cheapo tape."

Kissy Cat licked her paws and looked at the 7-11 sign like a gambler staring at a slot machine that just hit the jackpot. "Be cool," she said. "I'll get your scotch tape. Christmas is coming, and all the parents are stocking up to wrap presents for their kids. Little do they know that scotch tape is going to end up patching the oil pipelines in Iraq."

Deep Dan noticed a teenager coming out of the 7-11 and all of the sudden remembered that there might be a bomb getting ready to go off in his car. He scanned the inside of his Ford Fiesta with his X-Ray Vision glasses and spotted a few bags from the hamburger joint in the back seat, plus some french fries that looked like they might be explosive. Deep Dan dove through the window of his car onto the back seat and judo chopped a few bags to shreds, plus some french fries.

"You can never be too careful with fast food," said Deep Dan, as he got behind the wheel and peeled out of the parking lot.

"Man, the government is really on top of things," said Kissy Cat to no one in particular. "But I've got some planning to do if I'm going to deliver on this scotch tape contract."

Kissy Cat got in her Cadillac and drove off to her secret lair underneath the big oak tree in the field behind Detective Dog's house. The county had come in to lay some asphalt from the main road right to the garage underneath the oak tree, so Kissy Cat's car glided across the field as smooth as could be.

Inside her command post, Kissy Cat raised the satellite tracking system from the top of the oak tree. She turned on one of her many hidden cameras so that she could track Detective Dog coming back from the elementary school to Johnny Lawful's house. Dog was stopping everyone on the street and sniffing around for traces of Kissy Cat. He licked a few people too. That's why everyone around River Glen loved Detective Dog. He was so darn friendly.

Hmm, thought Kissy Cat, as she sipped a cold slurpee and sat back in the leather chair that was all scratched around the arm rests. Kissy Cat kept her camera trained on Detective Dog as she thought about ways to get all the scotch tape that the government needed safely out of the neighborhood. Detective Dog was the only thing in her way now.

Meanwhile, Detective Dog parked his Thunderbird behind the doghouse in Johnny Lawful's back yard. He looked out across the field and wondered what it was going to take to crack the case. Several of the kids from the neighborhood had confirmed that there was scotch tape missing from their houses. But Detective Dog needed to know where it all was going.

Suddenly, Johnny Lawful came running out the back door.

"Detective Dog!" said Johnny. "Now we're really in for it. My monthly research project on snowy white owls was vandalized. Someone took all the scotch tape off the pictures in my binder and the whole thing is a mess."

"Let me see that," said Detective Dog. He grabbed the monthly research binder from Johnny and put it under his trusty magnifying glass. "Just as I suspected," said Detective Dog. "You see these scratch marks, Johnny? This binder has been clawed by a cat that is part Siamese and part some other breed. You can tell by the paw prints."

"That can only mean one thing," said Johnny.

"That's right," said Detective Dog. "There's only one cat that can make paw prints like that. Kissy Cat is up to her old tricks and it looks like she's determined to get all the scotch tape in the neighborhood, even if it means destroying a monthly research project on snowy white owls. We've got to find her and put a stop to this menace before everyone gets a bad grade in school and Christmas is ruined."

As she watched the action from her secret lair, Kissy Cat had an idea, a very clever idea. She filled the back of her car with some army surplus stuff Deep Dan gave her as an example of what he didn't need and made her way around to the neighborhood. She was determined to get that scotch tape contract. And she knew that it would only take one drop of her own brand of kryptonite to make Detective Dog see things her way.

After watching Johnny Lawful go back inside the main house, Kissy Cat sauntered over to Detective Dog's house and paused in the doorway, looking her absolute cutest. She had that big pink bow in her hair again.

Detective Dog froze. Before he could get a word out, Kissy Cat slid over and kissed him right on the mouth. She kissed him hard. And Detective Dog licked her right back. He just couldn't help himself.

Then Kissy Cat unloaded the trunk of her Cadillac and sashayed away without saying a word. Detective Dog was in shock, beautiful, wonderful shock.

And Christmas and all the monthly research projects were saved because what Kissy Cat left behind was enough glue sticks for everyone in the neighborhood.

Picking Up The Pictures

Pictures speak volumes about our lives, saying more in one frame than an adult member of my family who is from the opposite sex can say in two hours on the phone when long-distance rates are at their peak. So I'm all for the camera and fourth-class mail. They get the job done a little cheaper.

That's because pictures do something words can't. They capture all the details from one moment in time. Not just the cheesy smiles and careful hair, but the kid with his finger stuck in his nose, and the family dog eating your passport while you pose in front of the poster from France before your bon voyage.

There is no better way to communicate than with pictures. They preserve the past and guarantee immortality to anyone who can remember to pick them up within two years after they've been developed.

Oh, yes. There's a time limit. I hope this is news to you. I didn't know the entire law on the picture of limitations until the day we picked up our family photos from the Christmas holidays.

When we went to the store and handed in our photo receipt, the manager came over to verify our identities and yanked the in-store bonus cards out of our wallets like a fisherman pulling his bait out of the water from sheer fright. It seems that we had been sent several courtesy reminders that our treasured family moments were wasting away in a drawer marked "uncollected" longer than the law allows.

I asked the manager about the retention policy for pictures, and he pointed to the sign that said 1-Hour Photo.

I see now how the door swings both ways. If you are going to demand that a poor grocery clerk get into the back room and somehow unravel and develop two giant copies of every bad picture you took using nothing but moxie, you had better show some respect for the effort by at least showing up an hour later to pay the bill and take your pictures home.

When a month passes by without the pictures being picked up, you start to get phone calls from the photo lab. "We have some lovely pictures here just begging to be picked up. Won't you please stop by today and retrieve your precious family moments?"

The problem is that the longer you ignore these helpful reminders, the lower the priority goes on your holiday pictures. When June comes around, Christmas isn't so important anymore. All anyone can think about is taking more pictures on summer vacation.

After six months, the photo lab starts to get clever. They pick out one or two promising photographs from the bunch that you haven't picked up, and send them to you along with a note that says, "Are you missing the special moments in your life?"

If they picked better pictures for this exercise, I might buckle under a little faster. But they usually send close-up photos of our dog Joey that show his eyes bulging out of focus and tongue wagging stage left following an unsuccessful bid to take the whole camera down.

I showed Joey one of these pictures to see if he wanted to pony up any money for them, and he barked like there was a full moon on a cloudless night. Joey didn't settle down until I sent the clerk back to the photo lab with a biscuit and an advance on his allowance. (Joey got one too.) I also explained to Joey that people are often startled to see how they look in photographs. But you can't avoid the harsh glare of the flashbulb forever.

When a year goes by without picking up your pictures, things get really interesting.

My wife got inspired not long ago and picked up several batches of pictures. She left them on the kitchen island. The whole family gathered around and ogled the pictures like archaeologists digging up evidence of a lost civilization. We passed around the Christmas pictures with particular glee.

But there was something about that Christmas tree and the Santa hat Joey was wearing that didn't look right. I seem to recall that this past Christmas we had the biggest and best Christmas tree ever, one that scaled up to the top of our living room ceiling. And I remember Joey looking a little cuter in that hat than he does now in the picture. No wonder the poor guy barks. We got the Christmas pictures all right, but they were from Christmas two years past, when Joey's hat wasn't all that great.

Crack Of The Bat

Baseball is the most American of sports. It has a long, rich history in our country, dating back to the late nineteenth century. So when we received a flyer for a boy's baseball team, I signed up my son right away. He's in third grade, and I thought this would be a good time to graduate from hitting tennis balls in the street to batting a real baseball.

The first thing my son noticed at practice was how hard a baseball is. He couldn't help wondering how much it would hurt to get hit by the ball. So I introduced my son to his glove. Your glove is your friend, I told him, and showed him how to position it properly to not only stop the ball, but catch it and record an out.

At the first practice, the coach was short on assistants, so I was recruited to help out. The coach showed all the boys the ready position, legs wide apart and knees bent with your hands out in front of your body, ready to scoop up a ground ball. My job was to hit ground balls to the boys and let them throw out the imaginary runner at first base. The training went pretty well, but I must have overdone my demonstrations of the ready position, as I scuttled like a crab from right to left and back again to show the boys how to range around in the infield.

The next day my hamstrings were so sore that I could barely make it down the stairs in our home. There's a reason why most baseball players retire before they're forty, and now I know what it is—they can't get in the ready position anymore without stiffening up for a week.

After the first game, my son complained that he had a hard time running with his new protective cup on. We didn't use those when I was a kid, but the flyer said we should get one for our son, so I did. The hard part was putting it together properly, since it didn't come with any instructions (real men don't need a manual).

A protective cup looks like a small urinal made of plastic. It comes with a special pair of underwear stripped down to the straps. In front is a pouch where you put the cup. The problem is that the cup doesn't fit in there very well. I finally got it positioned for my son, and he toughed it out for a whole game with his cup strapped in upside down. Now, anyone who is familiar with the human anatomy knows that has got to hurt. Of course, you want the wide part of the contraption on the bottom to get any real protection.

We got things reoriented for the next game, but because my son was one of only three boys on the team who even got a protective cup, his reward was to play catcher for several innings, a position he doesn't like. I think major league catchers must be victims of coercion somewhere along the line. Why would anyone want to be a backstop for ninety-mile-an-hour fastballs when the outfield is just sitting there waiting for you to lollygag about, chew gum, and shag flies?

In about the fourth inning of our game, the pitching machine uncorked a whopper and my son forgot everything I taught him about using his glove to protect himself. The ball sailed right for the target area at a very high speed and wham! It stuck right there. I know it sounds amazing, but if you turn a protective cup inside out and throw a baseball at it hard enough, it will stick right in there. This is sort of the opposite of what it's supposed to do, but an out is an out no matter how you record it. My son is now convinced that the cup is good protection, and every boy on the team showed up with one at the next practice. The coach even showed the boys how to put them on right.

The Case Of The Cagey Coach

I wish Sherlock Holmes was still around because I've got a great new mystery to tell him about. The Red-headed League was an easy case compared to the dastardly designs a parent encounters in youth sports.

I'm one of those lucky dads whose son is a good athlete and likes to play all the sports. We do soccer, basketball, baseball, and football together. Sports are a great way to really connect with your son. And your mortgage banker. Because you need a good home equity loan to pay all the sign-up fees. That part, I don't mind. It's the road rallies and Web sites that are killing me. Let's take those one at a time, and you'll see what I mean.

Imagine that you live in a town called England and your son's fifth-grade football team has a game in another town called Antarctica. OK. Here's your problem right off the bat. Why in the world does a ten-year-old kid need to travel to the South Pole just to play football? Well, maybe the game wasn't exactly in Antarctica, but it might as well have been. Or Timbuktu for that matter. When I got word that there was a ball game in a town called Sherwood not long ago, I didn't panic, even though I had never heard of the place before. Not me. Not when I had the whole Internet sitting inside a computer right there on my desk just begging me to look something up.

I got right on the Map Master Web site, and typed in "Sherwood" in the search field. Up came a map, with detailed instructions for how to drive to this elementary school from my house. Whew. Average driving time forty minutes. That's not too bad. One spin through Earth Wind and Fire's greatest hits in the car will get us there with a few songs to spare, I thought.

But the details didn't dovetail. The directions from Map Master got me out of the neighborhood flawlessly, but bucked me out of my driver's seat as soon as we hit Roy Rogers Road. Every car in the universe was turning left on Roy Rogers Road on this particular afternoon, but it didn't show up on the map I printed out from the Internet. That's when I had to make a split-second decision. Either keep going straight onto a road named Detour Dead End or give old Roy another ride like the rest of the cowboys on the stampede.

"Hi ho Silver!"

I followed the rest of the clues (and the other cars), and eventually pulled into Sherwood, minus my sanity but full of ideas for the Map Master Web site. First among them: no making up road names.

My son raced onto the field to join his teammates, while I sat in the car and meditated for a half hour. At least that's my story. I don't want people to know that a little thing like a road rally is enough to make me cata-tonic. I snapped out of it just in time to hear the coach's speech at the end of the game. Something about a team Web site he set up, where we could find the rest of the team's schedule. Goteam.com or something like that.

Now we're talking, I thought gleefully. I'll never need Map Master again. Not when I can print the schedule out ahead of time and get directions from someone at the gas station like a real man.

They wanted a password to get into the team Web site, so I tried the thirty-eight passwords I already have memorized. I've got different passwords for getting through the front door at work, logging on to my computer, checking my voice mail, and running the toaster in the break room. I tried them all and nothing worked. Even an English muffin with raspberry jam didn't help.

I finally decided that there was no way to jumble the letters in "let me in" that would satisfy this Web site. Everything I tried resulted in the same response: "Access denied. Prohibited directory."

But I didn't spend five years of my life studying computers at night school to be foiled now by a fifth-grade football coach with too much Web site security software on his hands.

Why in the world do you need to password-protect a Web site for a fifth-grade football team? Are the coaches from the other fifth-grade teams trying to find out our secret plays? If they are, I've got a little surprise for them. Every play is the same. The quarterback gives the ball to another guy, and then everybody gang tackles him until the whistle blows.

My boss found me slumped over my computer late that night, and patted me on the back on the way out because I was working late for once. My hands were curled into the fetal position at the keyboard, and my eyes showed the strain from trying to hack into the team Web site.

Suddenly, it all came clear. I tried making believe I was my son, and typed in his name as the password. And the Web site opened up like Fort Knox yielding to Goldfinger. When I printed out the team schedule in full color, I was, at last, a happy man. That was some of the best computer hacking I've ever done.

The next game was on Saturday, and I got there on time with no trouble at all. I had my schedule folded up in my back pocket just in case. When the nice lady came around to all the parents to hand out beautifully laminated team schedules to everyone, including the team roster with the names and uniform numbers of all the players printed on the other side, I insisted that it wasn't necessary. "Already got a schedule," I said with pride, as I looked around to see if any of the other parents noticed how on the ball I was.

I'm going back in tonight to find the team roster with the uniform numbers on the Web. And as soon as I solve that case, I'll know when to cheer for my own son at the game. The other parents are going to appreciate that.

Cast Off

When I broke my arm coaching my third-grade basketball team, the doctor put me in a cast and told me to come back in six weeks. He also recommended that I stop trying to dunk on the kiddie basket. Now, lots of people break a bone at some point in life and know what this is all about, but for those of you who haven't, here's a primer on how to get along with a papier mache project attached to your arm.

First, forget about your opposable thumb, that handy evolutionary trait that distinguishes man from lesser primates. With your thumb in a spike cast, your mobility is limited. If you are a righty and your cast is on your left hand, or vice-versa, give yourself ten points for luck in the face of adversity. You will be able to manage most of the everyday tasks that you once thought were easy without too much help from the nursing staff. And you will finally understand the Zen notion of one hand clapping.

But don't try to blow your nose. As you will learn if you are ever in this predicament, blowing your nose requires two hands with working thumbs. I never thought about this much until I couldn't position my tissue properly and missed the target altogether. My suggestion is to get rid of your allergies before you break your arm and steer clear of elementary schools. I've been known to catch a cold just looking at an elementary school.

Limit your workouts. This is difficult for me because I've been taking up yoga and found that a cast doesn't bend like a pretzel at all. And lower those weights, while increasing the number of repetitions. I've been using my wife's old two-pound dumbbells to keep fit while I'm laid up. That's what I'm talking about when I say keep your confidence up.

If you're tired of waking up grumpy in the morning, try using the cast as a pillow. This is similar to the ancient ascetic practices of denial and hardship that have been shown to put a dent in your head. Remember, external appearances can be deceiving and spiritual enlightenment doesn't come easy.

Don't shirk your lawn-care responsibilities. Instead, empty out your gas can and wander over to a neighbor's house where you know there are teenagers. Make sure there is a determined look on your face when you ask to borrow some gas. When your neighbors see your pitiful cast, they will quickly encourage one of the teens to mow your lawn for you. Be sure to have your wallet handy for this exercise.

When you're done with the lawn, you can take a well-earned shower, but be careful to keep your cast dry. Get a plastic garbage bag and wrap it around your arm until you can't see the cast anymore. Then hold the whole thing up in the air like the Statue of Liberty while you soap up and rinse off using your one good hand. Don't try to get under the armpit on the opposite side of your cast unless you want a matching cast for your other side. Just wave the soap in the general direction of your armpit and let convection and osmosis do the job. Gosh, I love science.

When the itch under your cast becomes unbearable, turn the tables and scratch your other arm. This has a reciprocal compensating effect for several nanoseconds.

If that doesn't satisfy you, take a steak knife and lay it sideways, with the serrated edge facing the area that requires surgery. Slide the knife under the cast and start sawing.

After you get the cast off and scratch your arm for a week, you can always put it back on using duct tape. My doctor seemed upset when he saw all the duct tape on mine, but he still used his little circular saw to take the cast off officially. Because there's no stopping a grown man who wants to play with his toys.

Below The Bronzer

In the big scheme of things (around the house), parents don't rate very high. I confirmed this observation the other day when I found out that my birthday present was below the bronzer on my daughter's wish list for payday.

It's not that my daughter doesn't love me or anything like that. It's just that bronzer is very important in a teenager's world. I never heard of the stuff though, so I went on the Web to get some inside information from the greater mind out there. I typed in "bronzer" on the search engine and got a whole lot of information that I probably shouldn't have.

The first hit was for a statue called The Thinker, by Rodin. It's a bronze sculpture of a man with his elbow on his knee and his head in his hand. Most people assume that The Thinker is pondering the great questions, like why we are here and is the universe still expanding. But I think The Thinker is a dad, and he's contemplating taking out a second mortgage so that he can pay for his teenage daughter's makeup.

The next hit was for the Bronze Age. This was in pre-historic times, when we were cave men and women, and just discovering tools. Men were using clamshells to shave and women were just discovering mudpacks, which were free. Things were simpler then. Ah, the good old days.

I continued my research into the meaning of bronzer and ended up on a Web site about the Olympics. I love the Olympics because they embody the best of what it means to be human. But then I realized that the bronze medal, good as it is, is only for third place. At least if you win the bronze medal, you get listed in the record books. The poor parents who come in fourth, below the bronzer, don't even go down in the sands of time, unless they're the quicksands of time. No wonder The Thinker has his head in his hand. Nobody wants to come in fourth in the family Olympics.

The next stop was the Bronx, in New York. I don't know what the search engine was thinking on this one, but I played along like I didn't notice the typo and discovered some very interesting facts. There is a popular female entertainer from the Bronx, and she has a new line of makeup out. Are you with me here? How much do you want to bet that bronzer is available in this line of urban hip cosmetics?

Even before makeup becomes an issue, when your child is just a baby, the bronzer is already at work. Yes, it all starts with your baby's first shoes, which parents like to have dipped in bronze, laces and all, so that they can remember baby's first steps in this world. Bronzed baby shoes are so small that it's easy to miss the symbolism, but upon reflection the implication is clear. Everything about your child is more important than you, the parents. If you have any doubts about this, go to the closet and get out your work boots. Now wouldn't it be cool to have them cast in bronze for all time? But that would make it awfully hard to mow the lawn, and you wouldn't want your neighbors to think you're showing off anyway.

So the basic equation is set in the baby's first year. They walk two steps and get their shoes set in bronze, while you walk two miles and get your shoes covered with dirt.

On children, Kahil Gibran wrote that, "For even as He loves the arrow that flies, so He loves also the bow that is stable." I like to remember that sometimes when I consider my place in the big scheme of things. Because below the bronzer is the foundation, all the parents out there working hard in the alchemy of daily life to raise children who will help make a better future. And when that bronze does turn to gold, we'll be in the winner's circle too. Then we'll all shine through.

Parental Controls

When the Internet connection at our house acted up, you would think we were cast adrift in the ocean, based on the reactions I got from my family. My teenage daughter doesn't like survival missions. She would rather go to the Abercrombie and Fitch Web site and look at pictures of other teenagers. Or text her friends on her cell phone.

But I had concerns. I wondered what evil lurks on the Internet, just waiting to ensnare young children like mine with promises of candy bars and makeup.

So I signed up for the new parental controls. This is a pretty neat system. You assign everyone in your family to an age-appropriate category. The computer then determines where each person can go on the Internet. When I was done with the configuration, no one could go anywhere.

I loosened up the settings under duress, but still managed to click on the check box that promised to send me e-mail about everyone's online activity, and information about all the banned Web sites people were trying to go to. The software promised that I would be able to investigate the suspects myself, and make a ruling on any that my children requested permission to visit.

I liked that idea until I started to get the actual reports. It appears that the programmers made a slight miscalculation when they allowed children to add comments and pleas to their Web site requests. The first one I got was reasonable. My daughter simply explained that she had to go to the Loreal Web site to help figure out her Christmas list. OK. That seemed fair until I got a printout of the entire product line attached to a big smiley.

And like the traditional twelve days of Christmas, the Web site requests that started with simple things like a partridge in a pear tree, slowly escalated into the equivalent of ten lords a leaping.

My daughter's requests gradually became more desperate in tone. The eleven pipers were piping, and I couldn't tell where the procession was headed.

"Dad. What is the deal with these parental controls? The computer won't let me go to the Maybelline Web site. Geez. It's just makeup."

"Oh my gosh! Not again. Dad, you have to do something about this. Now it won't let me on the Web site where they have the super-cute pajamas."

"This is getting ridiculous. What is wrong with a little lip balm?"

"OK. This has got to stop. When I typed in J Lo on the search engine, instead of the Jennifer Lopez Web site for her new perfume, I got a picture of Bill Cosby eating dessert. This is really scary. Isn't he from your generation?"

"Now Victoria's Secret won't let me in. Dad. Think about it. If the computer won't let me into the really cool Web sites, how am I ever going to finish my Christmas list?"

It took me an entire evening to review all the Web site requests. I clicked around until all the on-screen images blended into a dizzying mélange of clean-cut teenagers with great clothes, oodles of wonderful makeup, and super models by the bushel. I worked so hard trying to follow my daughter's tracks in cyberspace that I eventually conked out at the keyboard.

Parental Controls

When my daughter woke me up, I was in the middle of wonderful dream about sharing a bowl of Jell-O with Heidi Klum. Or was that on the screen? Either way, my daughter didn't approve.

"Dad. What happened to your parental controls?"

The Old Switcheroo

Bringing your lunch to work is a blue-collar thing that I admire. It was until after college that anyone could convince me to take a job working indoors. A couple of sandwiches at one of the estates where we were mowing lawns was my usual fare. Years later, I still pack a lunch for work, even though I'm in an office building now, mowing yawns.

There's nothing fancy about a turkey sandwich on whole wheat, but it gets the job done. And I'm staying true to my roots. So that makes me happy.

But the other day when I opened my brown paper bag looking for sustenance, I found a candy bar, some gummies, simulated juice wrapped in a space-age pouch, and half a bagel with cream cheese. The cream cheese was spread so thin that it looked like the bagel was just sweating. Aha, I thought! The old switcheroo. This must be my teenage daughter's lunch.

I ate it anyway, candy bar first, as an experiment to see how well I could do my job without any meaningful nutrition holding me up.

The results are now in, but I can't remember where I put them. I was too busy downloading music from the Internet and chatting at the coffee station with my coworkers to worry about that silly assignment I was given. My task list now features several creative doodles that would have shown artistic potential if I hadn't spilled my juice on the paper. And my hair is looking better than it has in years.

That night at dinner, when it was my turn to give a good report for the day, I mentioned my lunchtime adventure and raised an eyebrow as I looked over at my daughter.

I wondered if the cold turkey sandwiches did her any good, if the old adage that "you are what you eat" works both ways.

"How was your lunch today?" I asked.

"Oh my gosh, Dad! What do you eat? That bread had nuts in it or something, and the meat was gross. But the worst part was that you used the heel of the bread and put the sandwiches in the old plastic bag that the bread came in, all twisted up."

"There's nothing wrong with the heel of the bread," I said. "And reusing plastic bags is good for the environment."

"Not for the high school environment," my daughter shot back. "Do you have any idea how embarrassing it is to open your lunch sack looking for a candy bar and juice and come out with two gross sandwiches in a recycled bag?"

"But you ate the sandwiches anyway, right?" I inquired. "And you probably sailed through French class with ease, and handled your math test like a pro. The old switcheroo probably happened for a reason, so you could see for yourself how good nutrition helps you do your best."

"No, I didn't eat the sandwiches. I'm not a dork. One of my friends gave me a muffin. But I was pretty hungry when I got home."

"So what did you have when you got home? Something healthy, I hope?"

"A candy bar, some gummies, and half a bagel with cream cheese. Mom stocked up."

When I Was King

Six months ago, I could do no wrong in the eyes of my daughter. Now, nothing I do is right, and the only thing I can attribute this change to is the flood that swept through her bedroom recently, sparing the rest of the house, but transforming my daughter from a pretty princess into a snarling teenager. The flood I am referring to is also known around our house as my daughter's fourteenth birthday.

It started out like most birthdays. There were cards and presents specially picked out to please the princess. We lit the candles on the cake, and wondered what the princess wished for. We hoped it would be something we wished for too, so that a harmony of wishes could rise as one to the wishing place. And the candles all went out. The will of a princess is that strong.

Out came the videotapes from the family archives, and we marveled at how the princess has grown. Noted too, the things that haven't changed. The dramatic aspirations evident in costumes from Halloweens past. Jasmine from *Aladdin* and Arial from *The Little Mermaid*. Twirls in the foyer, mugging for the camera. Wedding dresses for playful dreams about a time far off in the future.

Then the cake was gone, or partly gone. There is no silence like the quiet that follows a child's party. The plastic forks and knives with frosting look forlorn, spent energy everywhere in the paper plates, mounds of half-eaten slices that started well, and wrapping paper all undone.

Can we slow down for a spell now? Change the direction? Go back to that once upon a time when I was king?

Ah. I seem to recall that I was a benevolent king who looked after his charges with wisdom, tolerance, and loving kindness. I handed out allowances every Saturday morning, snapping those newly minted one-dollar bills off the printing press in the basement with even-handed aplomb. I listened to the Z-100 teen radio station with an attentive heart. I came up with batteries for the portable CD player in a pinch, and fixed the gaping hole in the armoire where a certain ballerina tripped and fell into the door through no fault of her own.

I drove the princess to the ends of the earth on a moment's notice. OK. Maybe it was just down to the rec center, but I did use my new global positioning system to find my way out of the neighborhood. It could have been the ends of the earth, and it's best to be prepared.

But more than anything else, those were the days when I still knew what I was talking about. When a question came up about worldly affairs, I never spoke hastily. I thought about the ramifications. The situation. And then I spoke with the voice of experience.

And people listened. My daughter listened. The canary tweeted. Even the dog perked up. It was wonderful.

If I could just be king for a day once more, I think I'd pull up the drawbridge on the moat to the castle and issue a few decrees.

King to regain lost IQ points at will. Tune-ups every night when Jeopardy comes on. Household pets and other court jesters barred from putting their paws on the buzzer. It's better when the king gets the answer first.

Local fashion experts to show more respect for clothes that went out of style thirty years ago, especially those that the king has owned for all that time. Seniority to count for something in the royal closet.

Pumpkin of a car to look like sleek stagecoach at all hours. Who needs a fairy godmother when you already have a Rambler sitting right there in the driveway, and the power of a decree working for you?

Battle of the bands tonight! Led Zeppelin against Britney Spears and Christina Aguilera.

Impractical shoes to be stopped at the castle gate and returned to planet of origin. Fines for repeat offenders. Wanted in fifty states: high-heel sneakers with no backs on them. Whoever invented these monstrosities should be made to wear them personally. I've got just the draw-bridge to try them on.

Clothing catalogs banned within a ninety-mile radius of castle. Unless the words Victoria's Secret appear somewhere in the title, in which case catalogs to be placed in king's personal library. There's never enough time to study the classics, but you've got to try.

Curling iron to unplug itself when left unattended for more than six hours and promise never to jump in the bathtub at any time.

King's moisturizer to remain chained to the sink in the royal bathroom. No deposits. No withdrawals. This is a bank. Not a youth hostel.

But will that be enough?

Will people listen? Ah. That's what moats and draw-bridges are for. To keep people safe at home around the dinner table and having some good old-fashioned family fun. Discussing the pressing matters of the day. Away from the mall. And the Internet. And that nice young man who's been calling the castle every two minutes since the flood.

Horton Hears Us Too

I think my children are running some kind of shell game at our house. One day, you think you have enough toilet paper for a family of four on board. You even get nods of approval from the other shoppers at the warehouse price club when you roll out twenty-four bonus packs of top-quality tissue and load them onto the tractor-trailer. Parent of the year awards swim through your head, tantalizing you with the wonders of being a man who really plans ahead for the needs of his family. The applause is deafening when you close the cargo bay on your semi and hike yourself up into the cab. You wave to your fellow shoppers and head straight for your just reward.

Back at home, I get into my pajamas and turn on the lamp. Out come the reading glasses and magazine full of classic cartoons. Dad is feeling very masterly because he provided for the family like you wouldn't believe down at the warehouse today. But wait. What's that sound? It's barely audible, like in *Horton Hears a Who!*, when the little fellows were trying to get the elephant's attention.

It sounds like a cry for help. But what could be wrong in a house that is so well stocked there is barely room to get down the hall without knocking over the supplies?

Unfortunately, the sound is coming from the bathroom, and that's never a good sign. It's Horton! How the heck did he get into the house? He must have had to blow his nose or something. It's the "or something" that worries me, so I leave my safe chair in the den and mosey down the hall to see what the fuss is all about.

And there it goes again, but louder this time. This is kind of the opposite of *Horton Hears a Who!*, so I asked Horton if he even read his own book.

Horton said, "Sure. I read the book. But it was all about the Who's and the happenings in Whoville. Elephants have needs too. Especially sensitive elephants."

"I'm sorry, Horton. It must be tough when you give and you give and never seem to get anything in return. When you love till your love muscle hurts, but nothing comes back but more pleases and may I's."

Horton thought about that for a minute. I still hadn't laid eyes on him, because he had the bathroom door closed.

"It's not the love that's bothering me," said Horton. "Kids the world over love me to pieces. It's just that you're out of toilet paper and I'm kind of stuck in here."

You know, you go for a certain number of years and think that maybe you have a few things figured out. You know how to get to the bus stop ten minutes ahead of time. You know how to get on the service road when the freeway is jammed. You clip a coupon or two and get a manufacturer's rebate coming to you in the mail. You're an experienced person. The type of person who knows how to microwave a frozen dinner without even looking at the silly directions. But there is no get-out-of-jail-free card when an elephant decides to use your bathroom.

And this was not just any elephant. We're talking about Horton here. Probably the most famous elephant ever to come along in the land of imagination. The guy who saved the Who's.

I edged closer to the bathroom door and sprayed some spray just to be on the safe side. Then I heard the noise again. This time, the floor rumbled and the walls shook like we were having an earthquake. My picture from France almost fell on the floor. And that's when it dawned on me what this was all about. Horton didn't have a Who. He had the flu!

Luckily, I had my son's discredited walkie-talkies from Christmas still charging up under the drapes in the living room. The ones he said were interesting because they "weren't even on my list." I slipped one of the walkie-talkies under the bathroom door and opened a channel on the other one.

"Breaker, breaker. Is Horton there?"

"Of course I'm here," said Horton. "But what channel are you on? You're not coming in very well."

I yelled through the door to get on channel one, and we resumed our conversation, using the walkie-talkies to add an element of intrigue to the proceedings.

Elephants can be very reasonable people once to get to know them. And Horton has a lot of star power. But no matter how I changed the subject, he kept coming back to his health problems. I finally slipped last Sunday's newspaper under the bathroom door (no easy task) and that helped for a while. Horton bellowed and bombasted. He pontificated and pollinated. He sneezed and wheezed. Jiminy Christmas, I thought. The cartoon world is really starting to bother me.

Horton blew his nose for another five minutes. The walls rattled so hard that Horton shook the kids right out of their upstairs bedrooms. When they came downstairs, and I told them Horton was holed up in the bathroom, they got all excited.

I handed my son the walkie-talkie and he set matters right in no time.

"Horton," he said. "The toilet paper is not in there. It's all in my room. I'm making mummies for a big battle."

That's when Horton really showed what he's made of.

"Give peace a chance," he said.

We didn't need the walkie-talkies now. We were operating on a higher plane. I just wish I'd picked up a few more twenty-four packs of toilet paper at the warehouse store. Because you never know when a sensitive elephant is going to want to use your bathroom to announce something important.

Eulogy For A Sweatshirt

The intervention came too late. By the time I realized that my favorite sweatshirt was a goner, it was already mopping the floor in the kitchen and trying to dodge the dog at the same time. It's a shame, because I always liked that guy.

We met at the mall way back around the holidays in 1993. The sweatshirt was sitting in the window of one of the better outfitters looking like a good Christmas present.

I said to my wife, "Hey, look at the cool sweatshirt," and casually walked over to the store window for a closer inspection. It was a white sweatshirt, which shows a lot of confidence right from the start. On the front was a picture of a wood duck, a hunter's kind of wood duck, with a full-color nature scene in the background. And at the top of it all was a ribbon waving over the picture emblazoned with the words: American Sportsman.

Even though I'm not a duck hunter, there was something about that scene and those words that attracted me. Most of us like to think we are sporting types, and I'm in that camp. Plus, I love the outdoors, so I've always liked fresh scenes that depict the natural wonder that is still so abundant in this great land of ours. In fact, it wasn't until I got out of college that anyone could convince me to take a job inside in an office. And I'm ashamed to say it was all about the money. If I didn't have a wife and two kids to support, I might just go back to the caddy yard today, and happily spend the rest of my life smoking cigars and telling the younger caddies about the days when I could make two loops a day, back when it was really hot and muggy and they didn't let you wear shorts. Yes, that would be a nice way to finish my career. But as it stands, I have to live in a four-by-four cubicle and drool over the outdoorsy sweatshirts I see at the mall.

Well, the mall turned out to be the place yet again back in 1993, and Santa did not disappoint. When dawn broke that Christmas morning and we all went downstairs to see what kind of magic was afoot, there was even a box for me. Inside was the fabled sweatshirt. I'm telling you, there is no detergent in this world that can make a white sweatshirt look as clean and perfect as it does on Day One. It just about outshone the lights on the Christmas tree. Angels relaxed on the sofa, delighted to see such a happy scene. The canary tweeted. Even the cat meowed. Wonders and wonders spilled out that day, and I spent the next ten years trying to recreate the magic.

A while back, I heard a rumor that if you put a few golf balls in the washer along with your clothes, they ionize the water or something and get your clothes really clean. It's an atomic reaction, but on a larger scale, so I was trusting that the particle physicists had finally got this thing right. When I set the washer off, my next-door neighbor called 911 to report that my house was going to explode any minute. Well, that didn't happen, but the washing machine never really got over the beating.

When I pulled my sweatshirt out from the debris, it looked about the same as it did when I put it in, plus a couple of divots, so the search for the fountain of sweatshirt youth continued. Pounce de Leon jumped into the fray, but cats are no help with laundry, I'm afraid. And golf, I've given up altogether. I just don't want to be involved in a game where the ball doesn't play by the rules of particle physics. That atomic reaction should have worked if the third law of predictability was right. But there's just no telling what a golf ball will do. It doesn't matter if it's diving into a sand trap at the speed of light or damaging the internal mechanics of your washing machine. They just go their own way.

So I started watching television in the hope that the right laundry detergent would one day appear on one of the commercials and save the day. I even got ideas about some new plot lines for the shows. Now I'm waiting to hear back from the producers on a few things.

SCENE ONE. Today, the French government announced that the Tour de France, the biggest bicycle race in the world, would no longer feature a yellow jersey to be worn by the leader of the race. Instead, the top rider will be wearing an old sweatshirt with a woodsy scene and a duck on the front. Tour officials are confident that this will improve morale throughout the bike corps and inspire the riders to greater achievements. Vive la France! Gosh, I love the French. They really seem to understand a guy.

SCENE TWO. In West Virginia today, Civil War enthusiasts admitted that the annual recreation of the battle of Confederate Creek was not lost when the white flag was raised. The white flag is out and a cool sweatshirt from the mall is in! This sweatshirt is so good that it might turn the tide! Because there are a lot of guys trying to get a look at the duck and the nature scene and not paying attention to the war. Incoming! Everybody duck.

SCENE THREE. When the Mayflower landed at Plymouth Rock today, the people who were already living in America stood frozen in amazement when Columbus got off the Santa Maria wearing a white sweatshirt with a duck on it. Never before had the natives seen such a beautiful nature scene. And finally, the mystery of how to spell America was solved. It was written right there on the sweatshirt. Columbus got a lot of gooses out of that sweatshirt over the next few weeks. He caught a lot of flak for making a bad trade when he came home without the sweatshirt, but the original people already living in America now had a new way to mess up the anthropologists who keep coming around asking questions about religious ceremonies. The turkey has been mistaken for a duck in certain areas around Boston ever since.

SCENE FOUR. T minus ten seconds and counting. The intergalactic spaceship sits poised for takeoff at Cape Canaveral. At the controls of the spaceship is Captain Tom Buzz. But wait! Someone is on the scaffolding attached to the launch probe. I can't believe this ladies and gentlemen. This is totally out of bounds. Let's zoom in for a close-up. For heaven's sake, it's Tom's mother. And she doesn't have a proper space suit on. She's got something in her hand. It's a white sweatshirt with a nature scene and a duck on it! You can relax now folks. That sweatshirt is Tom's blankie and he never goes to Mars without it. It's all part of the show.

SCENE FIVE. Game seven of the World Series and it's come down to this. Two outs, and the score tied between the Dodgers and the Giants. Pinch-hitting for the Dodgers is Gabe Carruth, a long-lost second cousin of the bat boy's mother. On the mound is Gigantor. Folks, I don't know how a cartoon gets off coming in as a relief pitcher in the World Series, but once he took the mound, nobody had the nerve to challenge him. It's all up to Gabe now. He steps out of the box and goes over to the dugout to get a new bat. Wait. Hold on now. He's putting on a sweatshirt right over the top of his Dodger blues. There seems to be some kind of duck on the front, and a nature scene. He steps into the batter's box and starts running the bases without even waiting for a pitch from the big guy. Oh my! He's stealing home….

DENOUEMENT. "Dad, when are you going to get rid of that old sweatshirt? It's frayed at the cuffs, and it's coming apart around the neck. You're starting to look like one of those Shakespeare guys. It's embarrassing."

It was my daughter, and she was right again, of course. It's just that it was a special sweatshirt.

That night, something sinister happened. While the men in the family were fast asleep, my wife and daughter got into the hamper and pulled out the sweatshirt. I didn't see it for a few days.

The next thing you know, it was Saturday morning. When I came downstairs for a cup of coffee, I was greeted by the sight of my favorite sweatshirt, reduced to a rag and mopping the floor in the kitchen. When I protested, our dog Joey jumped into fray and wrested it away from the mop, but it was already too late.

Joey gets everything in the end, but he has no sense of history.

Mysteries Of Male Menopause

Doctor Blush began the lecture with an anecdote. He said that at a certain age a woman gets hot flashes in the middle of the night. She throws off the sheets and tries to get some air. She tosses in bed like a flounder still on the hook, perspiring like a sponge somebody squeezed over the sink. She tries to meditate and transcend, but remains trapped in a sea of mixed metaphors. Then at long last, when nothing else seems to matter anymore, she wakes up her husband and tells him to put out the garbage.

"Yes dear," her husband says, as he flips the pillow to the cool side and tries to go back to sleep.

"Why can't you put the garbage out ahead of time?"

"Honey, it's two o'clock in the morning. Let's worry about the garbage tomorrow."

"You don't care about my issues at all."

"What issues? Can I get you an aspirin or something?"

"I'm not going to take an aspirin. You always try to give me a pill. I'm just hot, that's all."

Doctor Blush paused for effect. "Now class, can anyone tell me the diagnosis for these symptoms?"

Someone in the back of the class spoke up. "Doctor Blush, I think I know."

"Yes."

"It's menopause, right?"

"Correct. But can you tell me who has the malady?"

"The wife, of course."

Doctor Blush grinned like a Cheshire cat, but didn't disappear. Not when he had the class set up like bowling pins for the strike. The students leaned forward in their seats. Then Doctor Blush uttered the one simple statement that revolutionized thousands of years of accepted medical knowledge. He said menopause was contagious.

I had heard about this menopause thing before I attended Doctor Blush's lecture, but tried to ignore the fact that it was going to spread to my household someday. I was already having enough trouble with my sinuses to worry about hypothetical issues. Then along came menopause. Once it started, it kept coming right on schedule, like a magazine you don't remember ordering and can't seem to cancel no matter how much you plead with your mailman. So I'm expecting a whopper of a bill one day for all this.

Menopause makes it seem like an alien has kidnapped your wife and is pretending to be her just to see if you'll notice. Don't laugh. Aliens might very well be cute cuties. We only make them look like overgrown bugs in the movies so that we can squash them easier.

Ah, if it were only that easy to stop menopause from spreading on the wind. According to Doctor Blush, the pods typically reproduce when they land on a worn-out husband trying to get some rest on the other side of the bed.

There was an episode on Star Trek a long time ago that had an empath from another galaxy. He could assimilate the hurts and pains of another person, so they felt better. Now I wish we never saw that show, because it might have given my wife ideas.

When I woke up at three-thirty the other morning, there was sweat all around my head and the nape of my neck. At first, I thought I must be having a nightmare, but I couldn't remember anything disturbing like you normally do when you have a bad dream. The window was open and cool air was coming in. I hadn't left the heat on like I sometimes do. My wife was sound asleep. There was no sign of a hot flash on her side of the bed, and yet I was right in the middle of a mid-life issue that seemed suspiciously like menopause.

How could this be? Is this what I get for casually flipping through Oprah's magazine after dinner the other night? Is this my reward for watching all those romantic comedies with my wife? Could this be what that darn yoga class was really all about?

As I thought about what to do with this unwelcome experience, I considered several remedies. I could get up and shave, do some pushups, and change the oil in my car. Or I could grab a few beers and watch *Die Hard*. But I wasn't sure that was the ticket at three-thirty in the morning.

It was one of those times when I'm grateful that I decided to continue my education by going to those University Extension classes once a week. I remembered Doctor Blush's lecture and hit my marks like a pro.

"Honey, did you remember to put out the garbage?"

Getting In Tune

O ne of the old Greek gods got in trouble for flying too close to the sun. His wings melted and they kicked him off Mount Olympus for messing up. That's about how I felt after I tried to hook my family up to the Internet a few weeks ago.

Coming down a mountain on your knees is never easy, but dads have to learn all kinds of myths the hard way. OK. Maybe there is no Mount Olympus in my study, but I do have a crystal ball with an imperfection inside. It's not the kind of crystal ball that you use to tell the future (I don't want to know). It's just a round piece of glass. Nevertheless, if you spin it around to just the right angle and look inside, you can see what looks like a mountain inside. If I turn the crystal the other way, I can make the mountain disappear. But even then, I know the mountain is still there, so I usually turn the display to "true" and start climbing again.

My latest attempt on the summit started when the siren song of the new Internet software put me under a spell. The packaging told the story. On the cover was a merry preschool child laughing at the ease of operation and wonderful new worlds that opened up to the whole family after installation. Sights, sounds, and technical difficulties were just moments away, and I couldn't wait to go online to join the fun.

Out came the trusty credit card from my battered wallet like a lightning bolt for the new age (Zeus would approve). That authentication software didn't have a chance. Just sixteen little numbers and an expiration date were all it took to install the program.

Things went well for the first few weeks, and then calamity struck.

It was finally my turn on the computer, and wouldn't you know it, up came an error message reverse high-lighted against the soothing blue background of the screen. It said, "An error has occurred."

OK. I knew that part. What next?

Well, there was also a culprit and its secret code identified on the screen: "Improper shutdown detected: 2114 5678 0156 0019." If anyone has a decoder ring for this communication, please give me a call. And no, that's not my credit card number.

The screen also contained some helpful hints. One said, "Press Ctrl-Alt-Delete." This command sounded suspiciously like the slogan for a sadistic software program with ironing issues, but I tried it anyway and nothing happened.

When the hardware freezes, go to the software, I thought. So I called my teenage daughter and fifth-grade son into the study to look at the blue screen.

I stepped away from the computer screen and said, "What do you see?"

My son said, "Dad, the computer's acting funny again."

My daughter put her hand on her hip and huffed. "Dad. The screen is always blue! And I've got a report due tomorrow. What is wrong with your computer?"

"Kids," I said. "This blue screen right here means that the computer is not happy. I wouldn't be surprised if a plague of locusts descended on our back yard or a lighting bolt came right through the window and singed the hair on the person who didn't shut down the computer properly."

I noticed my daughter subconsciously fingering her long hair at this point, but continued the demonstration anyway.

It took me a half hour to get us back on the Internet, but the Tech Support hotline was playing some pretty good Neil Diamond tunes while I was on hold, so I didn't mind.

Meanwhile, my children both went glassy eyed from watching me at the controls stomping my feet to "Cracklin' Rosie."

Once I had us back online, I said, "Be patient with the computer. Go with the flow. Tune in to the rhythms of the machine."

"I knew it," said my daughter. "The computer is slow. Is it from the sixties too?"

The Hanger Thief

A thief is at hand in the land. He comes in the night and steals the hangers out of the coat closet. Silently, he slips another coat off a wooden hanger and takes it to his secret lair. But what evil purpose could be behind this nefarious scheme? What hangers lurk in the hearts of men?

Simple things like coat hangers shouldn't require a lot of attention. When the birds sing in the morning, I don't have to put my thinking cap on. When the dog barks, I barely lift an eyebrow. When the bee stings, I just pull *The Sound of Music* out of the video machine. But when I get home from work and can't find my coat hanger in the closet, I get suspicious.

Besides, how many things can a coat hanger do? There can't be that many people who locked their keys in their car right in front of my house. To jimmy the window and open a car door, you need a wire coat hanger anyway, not a nice wooden one from a fine clothing store.

Could be that someone doesn't like my new winter coat. It is a little too big for me, but there's no law against looking like Elliot Ness when you get on the bus to go to work. The salesman at the coat factory said it looked great on me, even though I couldn't get my wallet out of my pocket due to the length of the sleeves.

People wonder what's underneath an oversized coat like mine. But a little mystery never hurts when you're looking for a seat on the bus. I might have a violin in there or a gumball machine. You never know, and that's all part of the fun.

Coat hangers could be collecting somewhere on their own and getting ready to hang a few T-shirts as an example to the rest of us. Maybe they all want to come out of the closet and move to Australia to audition as boomerangs. If that's the case, then they could be on their return flight any time now. I hope they don't all show up at once. Over the years, I have lost thousands of coat hangers, usually one at a time. If they all boomerang back into my life at once, there's going to be a problem. It would be like the swallows returning to cappuccino and finding out there's no coffee left.

But right now, I'm short a few hangers. And when that happens, I have to double up my many coats on the few hangers I've got left. This requires some otherwise unnecessary layering. My old, worn jackets from the 1960s that I never wear anymore because my wife hates them usually get stuck at the bottom layer, as undergarments for the new jackets I got for Christmas and my birthday. These are the ones that looked just fine on the dudes in the catalog, but somehow turned dorky as soon as I put them on.

If I'm not totally awake when I leave the house in the morning, I sometimes walk to the bus stop wearing two jackets instead of one. It's an honest mistake, but people don't like to chat when you have two jackets on. They cut the conversation short, give you a quarter, and tell you to make sure you spend it on coffee, not anything else.

Sure, I've got a few quarters in my pocket now, but I'd rather have my coat hangers back where they belong.

The hotels have the right idea on coat hangers. They put metal rings around the tops so there's no way you can take the hangers out. You have to angle them sideways and twist them around to get your jacket on the hotel kind. Permanent hangers. I have no idea how they got the hangers on there in the first place, but this is the kind of mystery like how they got a sailing ship in a whisky bottle that I try not to think about too much. The hotel kind also feature another drawback that I find to be hostile in intent: little metal alligators dangling from the bottom rung of the hanger looking to nip your fingers every time you open their jaws. Someone once told me you put your pants on there. Sure. Be right with you.

I once thought the solution to this problem was to just buy more hangers. No big deal right? How much can a wooden coat hanger cost? But when I went shopping for coat hangers, all I could find were those plastic ones that come in convenient twelve-packs. These things are so wimpy they can't hold my socks. When you put a coat on one of these plastic ones, it slumps at the shoulders like a batter who just struck out in the World Series.

Maybe a performance artist or a magician is secretly taking all my coat hangers and using them to make a bridge over the Atlantic Ocean. I wouldn't be surprised if I saw one of these jokers walking a tightrope chain of my good wooden coat hangers all hooked together and using one of those long poles to keep his balance. Like having a lot of wooden hangers is so great. Show off.

Safe Sailing

I worry a lot about my stuff getting stolen, so I never leave the house without first checking the intricate web of ropes, wires, and pulleys that I've installed over the years to ensnare any would-be thieves. It takes time to go through the whole mess, but when I'm done I can rest assured that nothing is going to disappear while I'm out and about.

I like burglar alarms too. I paid plenty for an electronic sentry, and I love to watch it work from the curb in front of my house. The key to the system is a little lawn sign which announces to any would-be burglars that our home would not be easy pickings.

While we were on vacation last summer, I came across an even better system, but I don't know if it's available to the general public. There's a wax museum along the waterfront of the coastal town we were visiting, and sitting in a window out front is an old salt of a sailor who looks so realistic you'd swear he was alive. Through the miracle of modern technology, he can sense when someone walks by and starts talking up the museum, trying to get you to come in. If you walk away without buying a ticket, the sailor dismisses you with an ominous chuckle and goes back to sleep to await his next victim. He makes you feel uneasy, like you're being watched.

That's what I want for my house. I figure if I charge admission I can eliminate ninety-nine percent of all burglars with one stroke of brilliance. (Talent shows early, but genius can hit any time.) Any potential thieves will have to plunk down eight dollars and start their robbing spree in my garage. Let's see. Here's a Lawnflight 3.5-horsepower lawn mower, circa 1989. It's not pretty, but by golly it still works as long as the grass isn't too thick.

Not in a gardening mood? Well, how about this sixteen-inch Little Mermaid bicycle? It's the perfect size for teaching children how to ride because it's so low to the ground. My son won't ride it because he's embarrassed by the little flounders and crabs painted on the frame. But maybe the thieves won't mind.

Burglars are not known for their patience, however, so I may not be able to delay the household stealing tour for very long. After the garage, I suspect we may have to head straight to the jewelry box or risk the possibility of having to give out refunds. Jewelry boxes we got! Come on up to the bedroom. Here we go. Ever seen so many Indian head pennies in one place before? They won't get you on the subway, but they're fun to look at. There's a few old watches in here and a couple of action figures that the kids gave to me. I've got a Hercules and a Quasimodo and whole set of Star Wars people. Don't be shy! Everyone likes toys, even burglars.

Not everyone fills up jewelry boxes with old coins and stuff, but I'm a little richer than the average guy. I've got two children who keep me stocked with basketball cards, action figures, and other things that they like.

The burglars may have a hard time pawning any of this stuff, but they're welcome to play with it for a while. We all need things that connect us with our own childhoods, souvenirs of past innocence or early dreams.

If that doesn't grab the attention of the burglars, then they're stealing in the wrong house. At the end of the guided tour, I'll just remind everyone not to run on the way out. It's easy to trip on one of the ropes if you're not careful. My old salt of a sailor by the front door can then chuckle ominously. "Aye matey, there's a strong wind coming up. Is everything tied down here?"

Yes sir. Next customer.

Fruit Conspiracy

Eating fruit used to be one of the healthful activities. My mother always had a bowl full of different fruits sitting out on the kitchen table when I was growing up. Any time I asked what was for dinner or opened the refrigerator door, I was told to have a piece of fruit. "It's good for you," I was reminded. Fruit always came highly recommended. So much so, in fact, that I would go to great lengths to avoid eating any. I reasoned that anything my parents recommended strongly must be poison to a teenager.

Eventually, I did come to eat fruit on a regular basis. I now insist on two pieces of fruit every day, hoping that the magical properties of fruit will somehow restore some of the youthful vitality that I lost when I was the anti-fruit.

In the course of this battle with the aging process, I have come to enjoy fruit. It does taste good, after all. I like the fact that it comes in its own wrapper. Bananas are particularly well designed. There are few pleasures as simple as snapping the top off a banana and peeling back the sides part way down the fruit for that first bite. Apples are good too—they're crisp. And the packaging is even better than what they came up with for bananas, because you can eat the skin. Imagine what a great world this would be if every product you bought at the grocery store came in a package that you could eat. It just makes too much sense, so forget about it. Apples are likely to remain one of the few commodities that can boast of this distinction. I have been reminded on many occasions that it is good form to eat the skin on a baked potato too, but have resisted. I can take good packaging just so far before I rebel.

In the fruit world, there are few items as challenging as a grapefruit. Someone realized this and developed a kind of spoon with a serrated edge—half spoon and half knife, I would say—just so they could conquer a grapefruit. If you don't have one of these handy, you can attempt a grapefruit by cutting it in half as a first step. Then it's hands on and look out because grapefruits are known to squirt inappropriately when attacked. Oranges are infinitely more friendly. If you get the good kind of orange, the wrapper comes off with ease. You just peel around a bit until the orange is ready. I have never tried to eat an orange rind, but don't think it would be a good idea. I did know a fellow once who liked to eat the white mealy stuff on the inside of the rind, but he moved to Los Angeles, so I can't report the long-range consequences of such boldness.

Kiwis are an interesting new fruit. They look bizarre, like little porcupines. Those are wrappers that were designed to keep people out. Sadly, nature's own defenses can do nothing to stop a person with a big peeler on hand. Kiwis must be peeled first and then sliced. This produces a limey sort of fruit with more seeds in the middle than most people need. I would put this fruit in the category of decorative comestibles; not the sort of thing you ask for on your own, but something worthy of a remark when spotted on a large platter, interspersed with other fruits at a party.

Peaches also have a fuzzy skin, but this is a soft fuzz. I never liked peaches all that well. When you get a peach open, you must first get out the pit, which is really a huge seed. If you like peaches that much, you can dry out the seed on a windowsill that gets lots of sun and then plant the thing. My dad grew a peach tree that way one time. It grew to full size, and despite the opinions of all the expert horticulturists in the neighborhood, that peach tree bore so much fruit one year that its limbs drooped under the weight of its own success. The tree died the following year, a testimony to the effects of too much fruit.

Which brings me to my main point. Fruit may not be as healthful as your mother said. Somewhere deep in the land of marketeers, word got through that people are not watching as much television as they used to. This caused a great stir that resulted in the idiotic idea to put advertisements on fruit in the form of stickers. I discovered this in the most painful way possible while eating an apple the other day. I took a bite and wham, ran smack into a small, oval-shaped sticker. It stuck to my teeth and had to be removed by a dentist. On the sticker was a small cartoon of an apple striking a happy uplifting pose. The apple had legs and arms, with big feet. His name, if you will permit me to state the obvious, was apple—Andy Apple, to be precise.

Due to the length of time that Andy was stuck to my front bicuspid, it appears that I will just have to live with the tattoo that Andy left on my tooth. A few weeks and it will wear off, the dentist advised. Meanwhile, try not to smile.

Despite the inconvenience of having a cartoon on my tooth, I was not yet ready to give up eating fruit. Having been alerted to this shocking new trend in marketing, I proceeded with due caution and soon came to discover that Andy did not act alone. Careful investigative work uncovered an accomplice named Bobby Banana. Bobby rides a skateboard on his sticker. I haven't found a sticker to prove it yet, but I think my mother may have been in on this too.

Getting On The Pot Pie Express

Just when you think things are running a little rough, you get a forty-cent coupon for a Pot Pie coming to you in the mail with no action required on your part. That's what's so great about America, the thoughtfulness of total strangers. I might just get on the Pot Pie express tonight and see if I can find any Hawaii 5-0 reruns on TV.

I need a classic retro show to go along with my Pot Pie, because these things remind me of when I was younger and really hated peas, until I ate a Pot Pie and someone told me they were loaded with peas. After that, I had more respect for the magical powers of Pot Pies and a newfound skepticism about heavy sauces.

There is a certain class of frozen dinners that has been with us since the Ice Age. Pot Pies are in there, and so are Swanson fried chicken dinners with mashed potatoes and a cherry cobbler. These were the original frozen dinners favored by cave men and busy mothers all over the world. And now that the Ice Age has been erased from the history books by microwave ovens, you don't even have to wait forty-five minutes with the oven on three-fifty to get your meal. Today, you get it express.

The best thing about Pot Pies is that you don't need any side dishes when you eat them. Everything you need is right in there. You get your peas, potatoes, carrots, mystery sauce, and something that kind of looks like chicken in very small bits, as confirmed by my electron microscope. And don't forget the crust. That's the best part, in my estimation. A good Pot Pie is ninety percent crust and ten percent mystery sauce, with trace elements from the other food groups. If they got any cheaper with the ingredients, they could easily call Pot Pies backwards biscuits and gravy. Innovation. That's the key to our success in this society. Biscuits and gravy is good, but you lose too much of the gravy when it swims all over your plate. Put the gravy on the inside of the biscuit instead and you're well on your way to a Pot Pie.

A lot of people seem to think there isn't much to say about Pot Pies. You either love them or hate them. But that doesn't account for the miracle of gradual acceptance, where you start out hating something, but then have to deal with it anyway for so many years that you eventually get nostalgic and sentimental about it. That's how it is with me and Pot Pies. They say it's the little things that make life worthwhile. When it comes to Pot Pies, I guess they mean the peas, or maybe the chicken bits, that make a Pot Pie delightful. So keep an eye on your mailbox and you might just get a coupon that rewards you for your patience.

A Tour Of The Museum

What is it about the refrigerator that mesmerizes our youth? Is there a party going on in there? Perhaps there's a hypnotist with a shiny watch who only comes out from behind the orange juice when he sees a susceptible teenager open the door. Maybe food is just getting better looking. People work on that, you know, the packaging. It helps with sales. But is it art?

When children are young, they grimace at most things you put in front of them, as if dinner were a daily test of survival instincts. They seem to think that parents are the people most likely to poison them (don't think about that one too much). By the time children reach the teenage years, they serve themselves an hour before dinner when no one is looking.

If Rembrandt and Picasso went into marketing, there might be good reason to take a long look at the contents of the refrigerator, but those guys and their paintings are already frozen in time. Meanwhile, the freezer is stuffed full of frozen fish sticks. Not that fish sticks are without merit. I'm sure someone worked very hard on shaping them to look like the smashed fingers of monsters that didn't eat their dinner. But that's not the kind of motivation our children need.

Last week, my fifteen-year-old daughter opened the refrigerator door and found a miniature Van Gough hiding in the lettuce. (Loving those promotional giveaways at the grocery store more and more.) He wouldn't come out, even after we promised to butter him up, so my daughter announced that there was nothing good to eat.

"How about a nice sandwich?" I said.

"What's so nice about meat?" said my daughter. "Do you know what they do to those poor animals before they get to the grocery store? They herd them into a classroom and bring in a substitute teacher until their eyes glaze over. Then they go in for the kill."

"It's all in the circle of life," I said.

"Oh please," said my daughter. "Don't start with that Disney stuff again."

So I got up off the couch, combed my hair, and put on a blazer. I even found the commemorative pin I saved from an elementary school trip to the Metropolitan Museum of Art in New York, and attached that to my lapel. (It's all in the details, museum guides.) I started the tour of the museum by yanking open the vegetable bin with conviction. Yes! There was celery for days.

"How about some nice celery?" I asked.

"Why does everything in the refrigerator have to be so nice?" my daughter shot back. "I'm tired of nice pot roasts, nice grapefruits, nice celery, nice everything. I'm looking for something with attitude, something fierce, something extreme."

"Look at these apples," I said. "They look like tough guys to me. And how about those bagels? They're straight from New York, with plenty of attitude."

"No. I think I'm in the mood for vegetarian pizza," said my daughter. "How come we never have vegetarian pizza or enough cheese puffs to last an afternoon? Didn't mom go shopping yesterday?"

When teenagers stare at the contents the refrigerator, they seem to be looking for answers to questions about life that the refrigerator just can't answer. It's true that not everything is nice and that celery won't solve many problems. But the stuff inside the refrigerator does change somewhat from week to week, and you never know when mom is going to strike the mother lode at the grocery store.

But do people appreciate the abundance? Well, yes. They know we're trying, the curators that is. But children are hard at work differentiating themselves as they grow to adulthood. It's all part of finding yourself in this world, a process that starts out with more rejection of what you're not than acceptance of who you are. And in the early stages of discovery, food that you see on the guided tour just looks boring, like it's all been done before.

One of these days, my daughter is going to get the idea and put something in the museum herself. And look out Rembrandt when she does.

Return Of The Jeli

I don't mind that I never get invited to the really swank soirees. I've got plenty of catching up to do with my collection of green stamps. But I do object when I get a reverse RSVP telling me that I've been refused admittance to something I didn't even apply for.

I got a letter in the mail the other day telling me that I could forget about joining the jelly-of-the-month club. I didn't even know they had a club for this, much less try to join. I do like grape jelly, but I had no inkling beforehand that people were on to me. Now, with no action on my part, I was confronted with the realization that I was banned from the big jam.

You might think these jelly people would have something better to do than reject unsuspecting citizens from their little club. They could have had a party and let people in. But they went the other way, and I feel like I never got my chance to join in the fun.

I never gave jelly a second thought before. If it was on a sandwich with peanut butter on the other side, fine. When it showed up on a toasted English muffin, no problem. But when I couldn't jar the door to the jelly-of-the-month club, I knew something was jelly well screwed up.

My mailman must have put me in for this. People from the postal service are always trying to help me in ways that I don't want them to. If I let it slip in a casual chat that maybe jelly isn't so bad, the package people get all crazy on me. I start getting catalogs in the mail from Lapland and other places nobody can find on a map. Special packages from Zaire (code word Current Occupant) telling me about secret plots to sneak the princess out of the country with just a teensy bit of financial help from me. Good thing I can't remember the account number for my Christmas club account without a teleprompter in front of me.

There must be some way to crack this jelly club. Because now that I've been rejected by the jelly people, I want in. What if I showed up at the local supermarket posing as an inspector from the Department of Jelly Control? It might impress the jelly club if they see that I'm really working the agenda. Bring me your concord grape, your marmalade, and your kind with bits of real fruit in it. Attention all shoppers. Lockdown in aisle five.

There must be a way to lift people up without using jelly. There are other substances that can make a person smile. Well, let me think. How about that marshmallow mix that comes in a jar. That stuff's all right. Tang is good. And Fizzies. Remember them?

Peanut butter is going to be a problem, though. It's too sticky. Without a dab of jelly to smooth things over, a peanut butter sandwich is a total flop. I think I'll send a letter to Jimmy Carter on this one. He's the one with the peanut farm. And he always gets back to me when I send him suggestions. If a guy can win a Nobel Prize by monitoring free elections and advocating peaceful solutions to the world's problems, I'm sure he'll have no problem reasoning with Jelly the Hut.

The Teapot Mystery

A person needs a teapot. Even if you don't make a lot of tea, it's comforting to see the pot sitting on the back of the stove waiting to announce the next quiet moment with a steam whistle. There aren't enough of those moments in this busy life we lead, so just the promise that the next one could be just around the corner gives a soul some cheer.

The problem is that when you're going on all four burners, the teapot has got to sit somewhere else for a while. And getting it back to its rightful place on the small burner at the back of the stove can be a dodgy bet at best.

We had a teapot once. It was a blue metal one, with a wooden handle so you didn't burn your hand when you picked it up. But then we repainted the kitchen, and before you know it the curtains changed color too. I should have known that the blue teapot was on the endangered species list at that point. It didn't go with the curtains, I suppose. But I wasn't focusing like I should.

When the blue teapot disappeared, I noticed a few pictures moved around in the kitchen too. They were probably in this together. But I had no idea where they made off to, so I called the EPA to see if they had tracers on any of these things. You know, like those little tags they put on hawks and bald eagles so that they can track their movements and make sure they survive from one season to the next. The people at the EPA weren't very helpful. The special agent assigned to my case asked if my wife was redecorating, and when I replied "yes," she giggled and suggested that I look in the garage for the missing teapot.

Ah, the last sanctuary. The people in Congress have been trying to get a permit to drill for oil in my garage ever since they found out that endangered species of all kinds have been gathering in there and closing the door. Something about national security, I think.

When I heard that Congress was looking for more oil, I scoured the garage and came up with a few half-empty cans of 10W-40 and some 3-in-1. I even found some Marvel Mystery Oil. I bought that stuff for my old T-Bird just because I liked the name. The T-Bird coughed and spit when I made her take the mystery medicine, but maybe Congress won't be so picky. I sent the whole batch to them FedEx, but I haven't heard back from them yet. There goes another tax deduction right there. What ever happened to the oil depletion allowance I read about in high school?

As I was looking around the sanctuary for the missing teapot, I suddenly realized that my entire apartment from before I got married had somehow been duplicated in my garage. There was the picture of Babe Ruth hitting a home run, and the 1953 baseball card of Eddie Kazan, who played for the Tigers. A couple of paintings by my sister, and the achievement award I got for participating in the medley relay at Prybils Beach on Long Island when I was eleven years old and going to the local YMCA summer day camp. One hubcap from my 1977 T-Bird, which I'm happy to say served as our family car for years. It may not have been a trouble-free car, but it looked great all waxed up.

There are also some framed photographs I took at Yosemite National Park when my wife and I were on camping trips long ago, before we got married. There's one of Half Dome that has a wisp of cloud streaking across the horizon. That cloud makes the rock look like super dog with a cape, a kind of Sphinx for the American West. Another photo shows Nevada Falls in the background, a reward, as I recall, for making it all the way up the long hike from the valley floor. My wife is sitting on a rock with the falls in the background.

After looking at that picture, I think I've got a suspect on the missing teapot mystery. I may not be much of a decorator, but I can tell when something has gone on the endangered species list. I just look in the garage. At times like this, I'm glad I'm not a teapot. I'm not ready for government protection yet.

Happy Birthday To You

I got a call from Western Union the other day. When I picked up the phone, someone on the other end of the line who didn't have my name right started singing happy birthday to me with all the zest of a Broadway performer who had just been exiled to an offshore production in New Jersey.

After the last chorus of "happy birthday to you," I was informed that this message was brought to me by my mother-in-law. I was to receive a mail-gram with a transcription of the phone call within the next few days. All to celebrate my birthday.

I couldn't eat or sleep until that mail-gram arrived. When it finally came in an official-looking envelope, I tore it open with eager anticipation. There were the lyrics I was searching for, nicely set in courier type with generous margins on beautifully crafted paper stock. The Western Union logo at the top of the letter was particularly impressive, as were the perforations along the left side designed to simulate the appearance of a telegram just pulled off the teletype machine. Somehow, the actual words didn't quite measure up to the impressive presentation.

"Happy birthday to you. Happy birthday to you. Happy birthday dear Choo Choo. Happy birthday to you."

My first reaction to the text was relief at learning that I wasn't just hearing things when the Western Union person breathlessly spoke the words "Choo Choo" into the phone like Marilyn Monroe introducing JFK at a big birthday bash in Madison Square Garden. But my next impulse was consternation at the thought that my mother-in-law still hasn't gotten my name right after all these years, along with the sobering realization that she has nothing in common with Marilyn Monroe.

The real mystery, though, is why someone would make arrangements with Western Union to place a phone call on their behalf. Why not just pick up the phone and call the person yourself?

It's like those big-shot mobsters from the old movies who never do anything for themselves because they're too busy cinching up their robes and puffing on fat cigars. When someone needed something to be done, something like singing happy birthday to a member of the family or bumping off a good guy, the big boss would never do it himself. Instead, he would turn to one of his henchmen and say, "Call Chicago. I want that creep on ice. And get me Philly. I want someone to sing happy birthday to Frankie."

My mother-in-law would have made a good mobster. She seemed to work from her bedroom at odd hours using out-of-date catalogs and a faulty memory to confuse the poor clerks who take orders over the phone.

At Christmas last year, she was determined to get my son a train set. The order went out over the wires to a small outfit in Alabama, where the accents differ somewhat. When Christmas arrived, so did four sets of trains in huge boxes. After we opened the first two and determined that they were identical in every way, we called the manufacturer. They pleaded with us not to tell my mother-in-law about the mistake. Apparently, she had them on the phone for a total of ten hours over a span of eight days hashing out details about what she wanted done not only at our house, but also in Philly and Chicago.

In response to each new discussion, the clerks at the train company did the only thing they knew how to do. They sent more trains. Anything to get her off the phone.

We ended up sending some of the trains back to the people who make them and giving one set to the local church. But before it was over, I had to talk to my mother-in-law about the affair. After a long discussion on Christmas morning, I finally got my chance to blurt out a question.

"What's with all the trains?" I said.

"What do you mean trains?" she said. "Those were supposed to go to Chicago."

Keep Those Cards And Letters Coming

E veryone likes to get cards in the mail. A greeting card is a welcome break from the usual barrage of bills and advertisements. If you're lucky, you receive a few cards on your birthday and on Father or Mother's day. Then at Christmas you really get a bonanza, lots of cards, some from people you don't even know. (I wonder about that sometimes.)

I was doing fine with cards up until recently. I got nine cards on my last birthday, a personal best. It's not as many as my wife gets on her birthday, because she's a lot more popular than I am, but hey who's keeping score?

I usually get one birthday card from my alma mater, another one from a local radio station nicely engraved with the signatures of all the on-air celebrities, and a few more from the car dealership and my real estate agent. That may seem a bit random, but a birthday card is a birthday card. They all count.

Then some of my favorite charities started sending me packs of greeting cards right out of the blue. Maybe they heard about my low scores on birthday cards. Who knows.

The trouble is that these greeting cards are starting to pile up. I now have a bunch from the Wildlife Federation that show photos of birds on the covers. I like those because they don't have any words inside, meaning I can freelance in there and write anything I want.

The religions send me lots of cards too. These all have words in them, usually along the lines of mini-sermons for everyday edification. Some of them promise that Father Jack or someone very similar will remember me in his prayers. Others have special dedications that will keep you safe when you're driving around in your car. Those are good, but I'm not sure where to send them. I wouldn't want people to think I was implying they need all the prayers they can get when they're driving.

Then the disabled veterans send me patriotic cards with flags on them to remind me that freedom isn't free. I may not know the full price for freedom, but I can tell you that mailing one of these cards costs about fifty cents. And it feels good to send one to my father-in-law, who served in the Pacific during the second world war.

I got a new batch of cards the other day that seem to be oriented to my inner child. There's one with a picture of a rabbit on the front that says, "Wish I could hop on over to say hello." When you open it up, the message continues with, "Being with you always puts a spring in my step." I like that one, but for the life of me I can't think of anyone to send it to. I do have some friends and family, but nobody has put a spring in my step since I fell off a pogo stick in fifth grade and sprained an ankle.

Another one from this series shows two bumble bees on the front and says, "The buzz is that it's your birthday!" Inside, it shows how one of the bees escaped from the front of the card and flew around the corner to the inside. This bee is looking at the remainder of the message, which says, "Hope your special day is sweeter than honey, with best wishes for the most wonderful day ever!" That one is the bee's knees.

The National Arbor Day Foundation sends me cards that show pictures of trees on the front. Inside, you can write in someone's name under an inscription that says,

"In your name a tree has been planted. You have been honored with a gift of a tree planted in a fire-devastated National Forest near Yellowstone."

I like the idea of giving someone a tree, but how are they supposed to get it home with those directions? "Near Yellowstone" sounds pretty vague to me.

Well, I may not have the tree, but I do have the greeting cards. That, and a few hundred others. As I ponder this abundance more, I think a huge collection of greeting cards might not be such a bad thing after all. Because I've got a chronic condition called life which requires more encouragement than I can muster on my own sometimes.

So keep those cards and letters coming, as someone once said. I'll be sure to pass them along to kindred souls with their own holes to fill. See you at Yellowstone. Not that I don't trust the National Arbor Day Foundation, because I do. It's just nice to see a tree with your name on it sometimes.

Something Might Be Gaining On You

They call it middle age because this is when everything goes to the middle of your body and just stays there, defying the law of gravity and probably offending a few fashion photographers.

It all starts as early as grade school, where you can now "charge" a donut when your parents are mean and don't give you any lunch money up front. I got a bill from our local elementary school the other day for two jelly donuts and a caramel twist, with late charges included because one of the donuts was stale. This is kind of backwards to my way of thinking, but I've learned not to question the new math.

Even if you start out skinny like I did, middle age will bloom you up. I now have a tire growing around my midsection that is so appealing Goodyear tried to buy it from me. But I said no way. I'm holding out for when they offer to make me into a blimp.

Meanwhile, I'm learning to like my newfound corpulence. I float around a lot better, for one thing. Now I don't need that silly yellow sea horse that takes an hour to inflate to enjoy my time in the neighborhood pool. This has come as a great relief to my teenage daughter, who is not as safety conscious as dear old dad.

The thing that confounds me is placement. If you have any doubts that life is just one big test, think about this. When you're young and desperate to grow a mustache or a beard, nothing happens. But when you're old and losing hair in the one place you never cared about before (the top of your head), it starts disappearing from there and goes straight to your nose and eyebrows. If my eyebrows grow any bigger, I might just take flight one day when the wind is up.

Same thing with weight. When you're young and have skinny legs, you'd give anything to fatten up the old calves. But after running in a few marathons and doing toe-ups for forty years, you finally tip the scales to your target weight not because your legs got fatter, but because your stomach just won the race while you weren't looking.

I guess this is good news if I ever have to travel across a desert and can't find a camel to haul my water for me. That's when a beer belly really shines.

I could take up sumo wrestling too. I'd probably have to move to Japan to pull this off, but it would be worth it if I could enjoy a second career bouncing big palookas off my immovable midsection. I don't go for those diapers those guys wear though. I may just have to start a new trend in the sport by coming out in my Speedos. Look out Japan!

When there's trouble in the neighborhood and we have to go to the drums to get the word out, I'll be able to just mosey out to the front porch and slap myself on the belly until I've passed the word along. My next-door neighbor already got the message and closed the blinds in his front room.

But I'm not embarrassed by my belly. It took me fifty years to grow this pumpkin, and I'm determined to enjoy the harvest. I may even lay down on the table at Thanksgiving like a cornucopia to liven up the festivities. The Indians always stressed the natural look, and I'm trying to stay true to tradition.

There's a new style going with young women who wear short tops so that their belly buttons show. I've never liked belly buttons much because they are such obvious failures. You could press on your belly button a million times before anything happens. And when something finally does come in, it's just lint. I suppose all the dust floating around has to go somewhere, but I figured wearing a shirt would protect me from this problem.

I don't like cleaning my belly button, because it hurts. There are nerves in there with long memories or something. You can't get the lint out without irritating the whole area. Now I know why the great philosophers warn against contemplating your own navel.

There are some things in life that go better for you the less attention you pay to them. Like how they make sausage and what the magicians are really up to on the stage. And I think middle age might be one of them. When it's your turn in the middle and the photographers come around, just smile. And don't look down.

Never Trust Anyone Over Eighty

When I turned fifty the other day, I realized that I was going to have to make a few adjustments. So I got a new bumper sticker for my car that says "Never Trust Anyone Over Eighty." People over eighty are very suspicious, to my way of thinking. I present here the evidence I have gathered.

People over eighty drive too slow, for one thing. This makes me think they might be casing the neighborhood for a heist that they'll pull off as soon as the ringleader can remember where he put the car keys. Or as soon as they deliver the pizza I ordered three hours ago.

People over eighty often wear disguises. My mother and her friends all decided one day that they were going to wear purple hats, and too bad if society didn't like it. When you get past eighty, you don't worry so much about what you look like when you drive past the local high school. But I worry. That's what keeps me young. The establishment may be frumpy, but they're still calling the shots behind the scenes. I thought I saw one of the presidential candidates wearing a purple hat and posing as a roadie the other day at the Fleetwood Mac concert. When I confronted the man, he claimed that he had nothing to do with the government. Sure.

People over eighty are unbalancing the whole country. They all seem to migrate to Florida or Arizona. Do you have any idea how this messes up the Electrical College? By the time the next presidential election comes around,

119

the Electrical College will probably be too busy holding courses on basket weaving to worry about who's going to be the next leader of the free world. Yay lanyards!

I think it would be better if we put our older citizens to work doing something useful.

One problem area is the stock market. There have been some shenanigans going on with the accounting at some of these companies. Let's have every grandmother who can still wield a frying pan march down to Wall Street and knock a few keisters six ways from Sunday. There goes your fancy deduction in the Cayman Islands right there. And no dinner until you come down and apologize to the whole family.

The grandpas would have their work cut out for them too, if I was in charge. It's high time someone slowed down the barrage of negative programming on television. Instead of these inane shows on TV every night, let's just give every grandfather in the country their own channel and let them tell stories about how things used to be back in the 1920s. I got your reality TV right here. Call it Pop Stars. We could have dueling grandpas tell their stories and let anyone in the audience who is still awake when they're done vote for the best one. (Look out for those summer reruns.)

I think this would set a better example for the young people in our country. Instead of kids wearing baggy jeans and showing the tops of their underwear at school trying to look like the hip-hoppers on TV, we could have them wearing jaunty caps that went out of style seventy years ago, support hose socks, and orthopedic shoes in the halls. Our schools would be a lot safer that way.

With the grandmas cleaning up Wall Street and the grandpas policing the airwaves, I think we would all sleep better at night. But our society doesn't treasure our older citizens the way it should. When a person's hair goes gray, they tend to get laid off from work and sent packing (give me that stapler back).

But with all these new drugs that can make you sing like Julie Andrews on a mountainside just because you went to the rest room, people can really keep on trucking (apologies to the Grateful Dead). As a result, there are now way too many people over eighty driving RVs the size of Rhode Island all over the country. Now I know why I can never find Rhode Island on a map. It keeps moving around.

People over eighty are ganging up at trailer parks and getting ready to take a nap right now. Their numbers are growing (ninety ho!) and they're looking for recruits. Next stop, a driveway near you. So watch out.

Obituary News

I think I finally figured out why newspapers keep publishing obituaries. It happened when I hit a certain age and I realized that other baby boomers might also be wondering if they will ever live long enough to cash in their 401K plans. I discovered that the remedy for this kind of negative thinking is to read a few obituaries just to reassure yourself that you are doing OK. Hey, at least I still have a pulse!

I like the ones with pictures because I can then read the story with a sense of connectedness, like I almost know the person. A studio photograph is often the choice, a picture taken early in a military career or upon graduation from college. The now-deceased person stares up at you from the newsprint as if to defy the fact that they ended up in this section of the paper.

There is often a sense of reproach in the gaze of the dead person's photograph. One can almost feel a challenge to make the most of the time left. I once read an obituary about a retired army sergeant, and was so moved by the story of his life that I dropped to the floor and did fifty pushups right on the spot.

Obituaries are like brief biographies that chronicle the major signposts in a person's life. Marriage, career, and volunteer activities figure prominently. It's clear once you get on that volunteer track, there's no getting off. Maybe it starts with an innocent invitation to join the PTA for an ice cream social. Before you know it you're running two scout troops and building a library on the side with funds raised through the sale of surplus wrapping paper.

An obituary never mentions my kind of volunteer activities. I am on the other end of the equation, being one of the people who buys the wrapping paper, and the cookies, and the coupon books for half-off dinners in New Jersey. You'll never see a person get credit for this type of selfless support in an obituary unless there is an official notice from the fire department: "Authorities found four truckloads of wrapping paper in the home of the deceased and issued a warning about the fire hazard."

When you read an obituary, you can't help wondering what your own will say one day in the future. About the worst that I can imagine is to end up with a one-liner that says, "Small-time drifter found dead." There may be nothing wrong with being a drifter (many famous people drifted for a good portion of their life), but to be labeled small-time is more than I think I could bear.

A memorial service will be held. Just about every obituary begins with this statement. Depending on your religion, this could go several ways. You might get a wake. I like wakes because they imply that you made waves and rocked a few boats along the way. Wouldn't it be awful to spend your whole life here on earth without changing anything or altering the course of destiny? What would they say in your obituary? The deceased never got out of bed and ultimately died from overexposure to *The Lucy Show*.

Near the bottom of the obituary page lies a small column of entries entitled "Other Deaths." This seems to be the place for people who have been judged to be not quite human. Maybe it is easier to find out who is an alien after they die. That's the only explanation that I can think of for this blatant discrimination. What if a member of your family turned out to be, shall we say, not of this world? (There are times when I have my suspicions.) Nevertheless, I would be the first to protest if their obituary appeared in the "Other Deaths" column.

Obituaries also include a few notes about the disposition. I believe this is a polite way of writing down what they did with the body. Now there are lots of ways to approach disposition, and many new techniques being pioneered all the time. You could be poured into a block of concrete and buried under the ten yard line at the Meadowlands along with Jimmy Hoffa, but that might require you to spend a lot of time making connections in Atlantic City.

The hot new trend is something called cryogenics, where they deep freeze you for a few hundred years in hopes that medical science will one day find a way to cure whatever it was that killed you. If you trust your doctor's great-grandson that much, go right ahead and get frozen. One day they'll bring you back and you'll just have to die all over again when you see the bill.

The Third Cousin Of The Pink Panther

I met a guy named Jim the other day who claimed to be the third cousin of the Pink Panther. He didn't look much like Inspector Clouseau, but I suppose our overriding culture of celebrity had to find its high point somewhere. So why not the guy who empties out the waste baskets at the software mines where I work?

I immediately suspected that Jim was up to something. He skulks around a lot and seems to have trouble handling even the most basic chores without falling flat on his face. So I had doubts about Jim's claims to celebrity status. I don't see many paparazzi when he makes his rounds, and he never seems to make the scene at the clubs in Hollywood. I think partying at the clubs and dancing on the tables is part of the package when you want to be a celebrity. I did see Jim dancing with the mop in the break room the other day, but his dance moves were so primitive that I doubt he learned his chops at any of the really posh nightclubs. He didn't get the floor very clean either. There were streaks everywhere.

And where is the nightly entertainment show in all of this? One time, Jim said to watch the show because he might be on. I put the show on the TV that night, but there was no sign of Jim. They didn't even mention the Pink Panther.

I'm not one to stand on ceremony though, so when the Academy Awards came around I invited Jim over to watch the program, figuring he'd enjoy seeing some of his fellow celebrities jamming down the red carpet in their finest clothes. But Jim claimed he had something to do that night. Could it be that he had a ticket to Hollywood all along and all my negativity and suspicion was for naught? Is it possible that Jim really was the third cousin of the Pink Panther, but had fallen on hard times and had to take a job as janitor temporarily while his agent whips up something good for his next comeback?

I decided to give Jim the benefit of a doubt and tuned in early that night to watch the red carpet coverage before the big awards, and what do you know? There was Jim sitting around with a few other celebrities nobody ever heard of and disrespecting the clothes the top stars were wearing. Jim seemed to have a problem with the gown being worn by one of the contenders for best actress. Apparently, it wasn't just unflattering, but dangerous in the sense that it could easily take a waif of a star aloft if the breeze ever picked up. Something about the billowy wings that were intended to make the actress look like an angel. Jim was all over that problem.

Then they gave Jim a microphone and set him loose on the red carpet. Before you know it, he gave one star a wedgie for not divulging the plot of his next movie and mussed the hair of the guy who was up for a lifetime achievement award. The stars didn't seem to mind as much as I thought they would. I guess there's a code among celebrities on things like that.

A couple of stars seemed to actually know Jim. He asked one star about some friends they have in common, and she was very polite. She even said that she kind of remembered one or two of them and might have actually auditioned with the second cousin of the Pink Panther for a movie that never made it to the theaters. Now that's validation!

This got Jim beaming like you wouldn't believe. They were whooping and hollering up in the booth. You can always count on the big stars to be classy. That's another part of the celebrity code. Even if you don't know what the heck somebody is talking about, you can at least make believe you do for a moment. It's the acting, I think.

These days at work, I give Jim all the respect he's entitled to. He may be emptying out waste baskets for a living now, but the guy has reach. He's done stuff, and knows people that know people. One of the stars almost said so. And Jim's fashion sense is right on. You can't carry on in a dress with wings unless you're truly an angel.

I'm Dreaming Of A Pink Christmas

A Christmas list shouldn't be too specific. Santa needs some wiggle room. And adding the suggested retail price to every item on the list seems presumptuous to me. But my teenage daughter doesn't leave much to chance. "Stick to the list," is what she told Mrs. Claus and myself the other day when she presented us with the directions. I was "this" close to putting the list in an envelope and sending it to the South Pole.

But Mrs. Claus prevailed on me to put some holiday cheer into my attitude. So I donned my 3-D glasses to read the list, hoping that my high-tech eye wear would keep the hot pink ink from jumping off the page and attacking my wallet. Those glasses worked just fine when I was watching *Creature from the Black Lagoon* the other night. I spotted the zipper on the creature's wet suit right away. But the glasses failed miserably in holding down the wishes on my daughter's Christmas list. It's a wonder there wasn't a one-hundred-dollar printer cartridge on the list, and a shame that you can't get one that prints only in pink, because that seems to be the only color that is required.

You may have gathered by now that my daughter is on a pink thing. Everything she wishes for is pink. She wants pink high-heel sneakers, pink handbags, pink lip-gloss, and a pink car. There aren't many pink cars to choose from, because most people don't have the one-track mind required to drive one. So I guess a pink car is going to have to be special order.

If I liked pink better, this might be easier to grasp. But I've always preferred blue. This is a boy-girl thing that starts in the womb, which is painted pink if the baby is going to be a girl and blue if it is going to be a boy. After that, your color preferences are set for the next eighty years. So it's not my daughter's fault that she likes pink so much.

I blame this all on a culture that is becoming more divorced from nature all the time. Blue, you can find anywhere. It's in the sky and the water, just about every place you look. But have you ever seen pink snow? I think pink is a color made up by some marketing whiz who wanted to sell more high-heeled sneakers to teenage girls. Or maybe it was Barbie and that pink Corvette that got us rocketing down the road to pink oblivion. In fact, I think it was Barbie who issued the first pink slip. Sorry Ken. Guess those pinking shears didn't treat your hair right after all.

If pink is really meant to be the color of Christmas this year, I think Rudolph will have a slightly different nose. With a pink nose, I'll trust Rudolph to cut through the gloom and lead me to all the things on my daughter's Christmas list. Then I'll relax by the fire and listen to some real Christmas music. None of that Blue Christmas stuff for me this year. I'm dreaming of a pink Christmas.

Special Report

We interrupt your life for this very important announcement. Today has been canceled due to snow. The Governor has declared a state of winter fun and is encouraging all Oregonians to stay home and build snowmen instead of going to work.

Trees are down, lights are out, and the world has come to a halt. We started announcing the school closure list at eleven thirty-five last night and we're still going strong. When we get to Happy Valley we'll let you know, but there's a feeling here at the news center that they're going to be delayed two weeks with the buses on snow routes that meander dangerously close to Idaho just to keep the plot interesting.

So put on your mittens, bundle up your overcoat, and bring out the sleds. When it gets too cold, trudge back into the house and make a big mess in the front hall as you take off your boots. Parents are advised to have plenty of hot chocolate on hand and the wisdom to say that the creation in the front yard is possibly the best snowman you've ever seen.

Let's go to Terry Travel, who is standing on an overpass near the Sunset Highway, for an update on the commute. "Terry, what can you tell us about the road conditions?"

"Traffic is so slow that it took two helicopters and a double latte to get me here. There's snow everywhere. It's snow, snow, snow. Do you remember that scene from

White Christmas where Bing Crosby and Rosemary Clooney are on a train to Vermont with their sidekicks Danny Kaye and Vera Ellen? They all look at a brochure and get so excited they start singing. Snow, snow, snow! Hold on. Now the snow's getting into my parka. Back to you in the news center."

"Whew. Thanks for the update Terry. Now over to our crack meteorologist for the forecast. Take it Bob."

"The barometer must be falling because I can't find it on my desk and I'm sure I left it here just a moment ago. We've got a lot of high-technology equipment here at the storm center and it's hard to keep it all sorted out. Hold on while I take a look out the window. Heavens to Betsy! It looks like snow! I'm going to go out on a limb here and predict snow all the way down into the lower elevations, with heavy accumulations in the news center parking lot."

"Man, he's good. Remember you heard it here first. The story is snow. Next up, expanded coverage of the tree that fell down in Tigard and an in-depth interview with a sixth grader from Beaverton who will explain why she likes to play in the snow. For those of you who tuned in expecting to see the playoff game, don't worry. We'll provide updates on the score at the bottom of your screen while we continue our special coverage of this breaking news story."

"Be sure to stay tuned after the game is over because we're going to go deep. Our panel of retired quarterbacks will discuss the history of snow and reminisce about how much bigger the snow drifts were when they were kids."

"But first, this update just in. We have a report of three snowmen coming to life in Salem and singing "Baby it's Cold Outside" on the steps of the Capitol. Startled legislators apparently had little choice but to join in the chorus, but privately many were saying that extending refrigeration and other state benefits to snowmen was taking the snow day too far."

"There you have it folks. There's no business like snow business."

Free Lawn Mower

Somewhere in the galaxy there's a lawn that suffers from neglect. Crabgrass grows where there once was a green expanse. Patches of dirt and dried out thatch dart a landscape that would make the Mars Rover pull up and call home before exploring: "Houston, we've got a problem." A hungry dog leashed to the front porch patrols the grounds, guarding against normalcy. Water is saved by the acre. Weeds wither and dry in the unyielding sun. And that's just the vacation house we're staying in.

I worry about gnarly lawns because, like moral failings, they seem to spread. They set a bad precedent. When a friend joked years ago that he wanted to pave over his front yard and paint the asphalt green, I recoiled at the thought, but now I'm thinking green is good. Anything would be an improvement over the science experiment gone haywire that I see now. If dandelions and crabgrass were ever going to mate and create a new strain of man-killing weed, it would happen right here.

The pods could spread with the wind and evolve, eventually taking over people's bodies like they did in those old science fiction movies from the 1950s. ("Don't fight it Jim, They're here to help us.")

People with unkempt yards are one thing, but when their eyes glaze over and they start talking about the futility of resistance, I get a little scared.

My own lawn now has enough fertilizer on it to last for fifty years, and I'm pumping on the water like I owned the Great Lakes. I'll do anything to keep the pods from taking over my brain. If an over-groomed lawn is the price to pay for membership in a free society, then I'm going to mow and trim until Good Housekeeping comes over to slap their seal of approval on my garden shears and pull all the casseroles out of my refrigerator.

Sad lawns seem to be leading indicators of discontent. I have yet to meet a person with a weedy lawn who was happy with his life. The sadness shows in the broken-down cars up on cinder blocks on the side of the house, awaiting a brake job that will never come. It sounds from the scraggly trees, where unfriendly crows screech like crooked forks scraping a rusty skillet. When I hear their obnoxious wake-up call, I cringe and think how nice it would be if they would at least try the mouthwash I gave them for Christmas.

Maybe the community can help stop this epidemic of slacker lawns. The lawn police could put out an all-points bulletin when they see a lawn going bad. "Calling all lawn mowers. We've got a doozy here." The neighbors could assemble with their weed whackers and a convoy of riding mowers for an inspiration march that circles the block with horns blaring and signs waving about hope for civilization.

Like the spirited barn-raisings of old that brought people together to help one another, we could finish up with a ceremonial lawn mowing to show how it's done, followed by a celebration barbecue, a few spins of "We Are Family" on the boom box, and a soda pop or two.

But I'm not sure a neighborhood party will work. The trouble is that people with bad lawns rarely make the connection between their weeds and their other problems in this world. The concept of cause and effect seems to be lost on them. But it's never too late to start shaping your own lawn's destiny. Mowing the lawn may be its own reward, but when you're done, you can't help feeling better about your lot in life.

As we were packing up to go home after our restful vacation worrying about the poor people who live in this place year-round, I spotted a for-sale sign tacked to the wall in the garage. Here's what it said.

<u>Free Lawn Mower</u>
1989 Ferrari-red rotary lawn mower
3.5-HP Briggs & Stratton engine
148 cc displacement (non-temporal)
65.09 mm bore (hum to overcome)
44.45 mm stroke (only affects frontal lobe)
4 adjustable wheels (permanently adjusted)
Easy-overflow gas tank
Bag in back (fills quickly)
Automatic intermittent shutoff
Pull cord (for tennis elbow)
Cute goggles (not appropriate for night vision)
High mileage
No brakes
Noise pollution below pain threshold (scares moles)
Sky-high hydrocarbon emissions
Current owner moving to Iceland

The New Wheel

I like to reinvent the wheel. It's always a good idea to think for yourself, and just imagine how much creative fun you can have if you pay no attention to the inventors who actually discovered things first.

I started out on cheese dogs and worked my way up from there. The cheese dog is one of those American classics that you just don't want to be without. Start with a regular hot dog, and slice it lengthwise. Then cut some thin slivers of cheddar or American cheese and lay them in the gap. Put the whole mess in a frying pan on low heat and cover. Then keep a lookout for fires. If you don't see flames leaping out the side of the pan in the next minute or two, you're in luck. Remove the cover and enjoy!

When I first invented the cheese dog, I was so proud of myself that I told everyone in my family about it. My parents immediately filed an injunction, because they thought someone else might have actually cooked a cheese dog before I did, but nobody ever hassled Columbus about discovering America just because a few people were already living here when he arrived. The judge wasn't real interested in this particular lesson on American history, but he did get excited when I started a fire in court using Exhibit A. Darn Bunsen burners. They work just fine in chemistry class when you're singing all the hair off your eyebrows, but when you try to cook a cheese dog on the fly they flame out on you.

I screamed out, "Hold the mayo" after I finally got the fire started, but they dragged me off to Hot Dog Island to serve my time anyway. You would not believe the imposters you run into in a low-security prison. There wasn't one good cook in the lot.

The moral of the story is to not let anyone spoil your fun with prior claims to greatness. The march of science is not very impressive when there's only one person in the parade. It takes a village. And a Snoopy float wouldn't hurt. Go all out.

I want everyone who discovered all on their own that you can drink water right out of a hose without bothering with a glass, to take a good long sip and be glad nobody put a meter on the hose and tried to charge you royalties for cooling off on a hot summer day.

There once was a guy in Marin County, California, who discovered that you don't need to eat any food to survive. All you need to do is breathe the right way and you're all set. The air is just loaded with little nutrients that are invisible to the naked eye, was the theory. This fellow was dangerously thin, but a lot of people liked him until he was spotted wolfing down a Twinkie behind the stage door at one of his seminars. Hey, you can't blame a guy for trying. And it was a beautiful, if flawed, hypothesis.

It's better to invent something with real substance, but be careful. There are a lot of dead inventors at the bottom of the Grand Canyon. I like a leap of faith as well as the next guy, but leaping out of bed in the morning is dangerous enough for me.

If you want to stay in one piece, get a good football helmet and just hang around thinking about stuff. Deep stuff. Important equations. Just think how many football helmets Isaac Newton could have sold after he discovered gravity if he was properly equipped that day when he was sitting under the apple tree trying to take a nap and got bonked on the head by an apple. Look to the great ones for your inspiration!

And while you're turning that one over in your mind, consider how much easier life would have been for the average prehistoric man if he had monster truck tires on his car instead of those silly rocks cut into squares. The Flintstone family car may look good in the movies, but that's all special effects. If we had been satisfied with the first wheel and stopped reinventing it every year, we'd be in a real pickle today on the freeway.

Paid Advertisement

Everybody gets gas, but no one likes to pay for it. That's why I invented the fartmobile. Why pay good money to the gas companies for something you can produce on your own using nothing but a burrito and a bag of chips? These oil barons have been ripping us off for years by selling us dinosaur by-products and making tasteless jokes about our own capacity to generate methane.

There has always been something suspicious about the idea that we should be embarrassed about a natural bodily function. People don't laugh when you're eating, drinking, or breathing. When things come into our bodies, it's not funny. But when anything comes back out, we all get hysterical. You can blame this all on the oil companies who are trying to convince us that our own gas isn't up to snuff.

We all have it within ourselves to motor anywhere we want using our own fuel, but society has always frowned upon the fart. That's all going to change now that dinosaur gas is up to a zillion dollars a gallon and still rising.

Don't tell your neighbors, because I want to make some money on this, but it's easy to convert your existing car into a fartmobile. You just pull out the front seat, stick a toilet in there, and dress it up with a plush velvet cover.

Then you sit in the car and wait for ignition. On the maiden voyage of my prototype car, it took me two hours to get out of the driveway using this method of propulsion, but I'm not done fine tuning the gears.

Fartmobiles perform particularly well going downhill. In fact, there's no stopping them on a steep slope. A stiff breeze helps too. I like a windy day myself, because it gets me in a carefree mood that's just right internal combustion.

These cars are good for the environment because they help protect the ozone layer. That's why you'll get a tax credit for recycling when you buy one. If you simply let your farts go their own way, they invariably head straight for the person next to you and then soar up into the ozone, where they stay trapped in a giant cloud. That's why NASA doesn't let astronauts smoke. If one of them ever tossed a match into that cloud on the way to the moon, we'd have the mother of all gas grills going in the sky and nothing to barbecue but ourselves.

For those times when you're driving but not feeling fired up, we have a tasty little contraption called a past-wind. It looks a lot like an old soda pop bottle, but don't get any ideas. This is a high-technology piece of equipment. The past-wind is free for a limited time when you buy a new fartmobile.

We'd have a lot less accidents on the nation's highways if everyone would just try one of my alternative cars. They putter along at top speeds of about fifteen miles an hour and smell so unusual that other motorists give you plenty of room on the road.

You bicycle riders are in luck too. I'm working on a modified engine that you can strap right onto your seat. Instead of pumping your legs to get around, you just eat a big breakfast and wait for the power surge. It's a breathtaking sight. You might want to think about fireproof pants if you go with the bike version.

If you really want a thrill, try our four-seater sedan. This takes a little teamwork, but there is no end to the fun when you and your friends are hitting on all four cylinders. Look out!

At the next OPEC meeting, I hope our government leaders let the oil producers know that we are not without alternative sources of fuel. When the subject of oil prices comes up, I've instructed the president to let er rip. This may seem like an appalling breach of protocol, but it's important to remind the world that America is a country with plenty of gas.

Take The Money And Fun

"And for our special guest tonight here on Swell Street Week, we have a man who is equally at home raiding cookie jars and making withdrawals at some of the biggest banks on the New York Stock Exchange. As special advisor to the loosely held Future Fund, the decisions he makes affect the retirement plans of at least two baby boomers. So it is with great pleasure that I introduce Ral Highcart."

"Welcome, Ral. Please have a seat."

"Thanks, Lou. Always a pleasure."

"Ral. A lot of people are stressed about the low interest rates they're earning on their CDs and money market funds. Is there any hope for the fixed-income investors out there?"

"Lou, let's do the math. One potato, two potato. No hold on, we need the new math for this. Let's see. The present value of one hundred dollars discounted for inflation and adjusted for taxes is about a hundred bucks. If you try to amortize this over the lifetime of your mortgage, you'll probably be dead before you'll ever see that money again. But if you leave it in the mattress, you get a lumpy bed. We call this poor distribution across the investment horizon. It leads to back problems and insomnia."

"So what does the average guy do in this low-rate environment?"

"You take the money, Lou. And fun."

"I assume you mean fun in the figurative sense. So where do you put all that money? I mean, where are you going to get the kind of returns that will cover your spread?"

"Forget about covering the spread," Lou. "You could put the whole country on low-carb margarine and still not fit into those new slackers with a pinch more room in the cheeks and thigh. Plus, you get a lousy sandwich that way. I'm talking about stuffing your bazookas into hot tubs, motorboats, and fancy cars. Let it all hang out."

"But what about sound retirement planning, Ral? Don't you think the average investor should be putting every penny into mutual funds and trusting the smart guys on Swell Street to invest it wisely?"

"Have you got a calculator, Lou? Let me show you something. If you listen to the experts there's no way you're ever going to retire. You could live on baked beans and oatmeal for forty years and still not have enough money to jump ship."

"I happen to like baked beans, Ral."

"No kidding, Lou. Ever play chicken? When we were kids, we would sometimes stand on the railroad tracks and see who could stay there the longest before jumping to the side to avoid the train. Imagine forty million baby boomers all waiting on the railroad tracks to see how much money they can make in the stock market before they jump off to avoid the crash. You can't have everybody diving for cover at the same time. There's going to be collisions. This will be the biggest game of chicken you ever saw. My advice is to get off the tracks and onto the train."

"Ral, you seem to speak in metaphors a lot."

"All the wise ones do, Lou. It's easier to make money that way. Love train, soul train, peace train. They're all good."

"Let's be more specific, Ral. How does a baby boomer get off the tracks and onto the train?"

"Become a CEO or buy an Al Green album. Anything to stay out of the clinker."

"Ral. What do you say to people who want to retire early? How do you do it?"

"It's all mental, Lou. Plus it takes a few bucks. Sell your stock while you still can and fly to the Bahamas to celebrate. Don't forget your shorts and shades. Retirement isn't something that happens when you quit your job. It's a relaxed state of mind. Take the money and fun."

Help Me Rhonda

I always imagined that the Bureau of Control would be located in an underground bunker half the size of Kentucky or cleverly disguised in the back of a tailor shop on the upper east side of Manhattan. A place where men in trench coats slip into the shop and disappear into a dressing room with a hidden revolving door. So I was shocked when they sent me a letter and made the tactical error of including a return address. As it turns out, the bureau is actually located in a P.O. Box in Albuquerque, New Mexico.

The letter that tipped me off wasn't really necessary. It was just another credit card offer, and I've already got plenty of those. That's why I'm certain it was some sort of rookie mistake, a fabulous blunder that threatens to unwind the tightly wound veil of secrecy that surrounds the government's clandestine efforts to monitor everyday citizens like you and me.

Oh sure, I thought. This credit card is probably rigged with more scanners and tracking chips than the White House. And now they want me to call their 1-800 number? They must want to take a recording so that they can synthesize my voice and use their hi-tech equipment to order commemorative plates and die-cast replicas of old cars for their own use. (Someone must be buying those commemorative plates.)

But after getting so close to the Bureau of Control, I couldn't resist the lure of a toll-free call that could lead to more inside information. So, I dialed the number carefully and a woman named Rhonda answered the phone. She was very polite. Almost too polite, if you know what I mean. She claimed that she worked for a bank, but I knew better.

I tried to stall for time, time to think up a better plan, but Rhonda went straight for my social security number. Whoa! That's the key to every database in Wisconsin, and other states. But Rhonda's voice sounded nice, so I gave her the number anyway.

That's when Rhonda started to get really personal. She wanted to know my mother's maiden name. For security purposes. I caved in like a mine shaft built with popsicle sticks and coughed up the name. It was no use resisting the smooth advances of this professional agent.

She's probably a Rhodes Scholar, I thought. Someone who graduated from Yale and was secretly recruited by the CIA to work the front lines at the Bureau of Control. I was helpless to resist the remaining portion of the interrogation.

Then, just when I felt like we were starting to make a real connection, Rhonda activated my credit card and told me to hang up.

Now every time I charge something I can't afford, I think of Rhonda and the Bureau of Control. I know they're listening. But I can't seem to stop spending and singing.

"Help me Rhonda. Help, help me Rhonda."

Let It Go Yoga

I finally found a way to do yoga that shortens up the path to enlightenment. You just lie on your back with your arms at your sides and palms facing upwards ready to receive inspiration and peace. Be still and breathe deeply. Imagine that your breath is the sound of the ocean, slowly drowning you.

No, wait. Wake up. I mean, imagine that your breath is a straw and the air is pure oxygen. You're on a space mission and your tank is full. Floating freely in outer space forever, with no way to stop. Just gliding around in the stars for years on end until....

Hold on. Back to the space ship. You're a kite flying high over the field at the local elementary school. A carefree child has a good grip on the string holding you to the ground. The high-tension electrical wires nearby don't pose a threat because we're all electrical beings anyway. Put your trust in the fifth grader who's not watching where you're going and ZAP. You just caused a blackout in the tri-county area. But you may be the most enlightened piece of instant beef jerky ever seen in the annals of yoga.

See how easy it is to leave your worries behind? All it takes is a little imagination and proper breathing techniques. Possibly a sticky mat too. Just to keep you from floating away.

When I first started doing yoga, I wasn't searching for enlightenment. I was looking for a way to cure my aching back. After helping a friend move three hundred boxes of Beanie Babies from his old garage to his new one, I sat down on one of the boxes and never got up. My back just wouldn't straighten out anymore. And it hurt. But the physical pain was nothing compared to the humiliation I endured when my friend's wife attached a heart-shaped tag to my ear and put me in a box labeled "not ready to retire."

I did a lot of good thinking in that box. In particular, I thought about Yoda, how he moved space ships in Star Wars using nothing but the power of his mind (plus the force). I wanted to be able to do that on a small scale, starting with moving that box off my head. And then I was going to go for the whole magilla. Deft moves with light sabers, leading the rebel forces to victory over the evil empire, and getting out of bed in the morning without a winch.

So I got one of those yoga exercise videos. I watched it all the way through the first time as Gumby stretched and contorted in ways that only a cartoon can. I tried doing that for a while, but soon realized that you can't be a small stuffed animal and a cartoon character all in one lifetime. I had to be me. So I waited for the cool-down exercises at the end of the video and finally hit pay dirt.

Gumby said to lie down on your back and turn your palms open to the heavens. Then he instructed us to empty our pockets of all material possessions and give him our credit card numbers. In return, we would receive a sticky mat and a special poem. Something to keep us grounded on our journey to enlightenment. That was the day I learned how to let it go, and I owe it all to yoga. I may be a little over-extended now, but I can bend and stretch like you wouldn't believe.

I went back to the scene of the crime to show my friend how well I recuperated from the Beanie Baby move, and read everyone my new poem. My friend's wife was so impressed that she attached a new heart-shaped tag to my ear and said they just might retire me yet.

Summer Doesn't Last Forever

S ummer is the longest season by far. It stretches from the dewy mornings of early June right up through the first day of the new school year. In between, lie the shifting sands of sweltering hot afternoons and curious children exploring the desert days of not doing. God save the bugs. God save the parents. How will we ever escape from summer, and who'll make the lemonade when we're gone?

But we're not gone. Didn't make it to Europe (again) this year, but wanted to dream about it just a bit. The travel agent knows the type of family that summers overseas and it's not us. So we settled for sidewalk bistros butting up against our own front yard. The drinks are too much. Not the fifty cents, steep as it may seem, but the sugar. I wondered where all the sugar for my coffee went.

Turns out that I'm the only customer so far, so the kids can't change a dollar. I know. I'll just buy two rounds. But then how will the children split the take? I can't be expected to figure out everything.

Like how to catch grasshoppers. You see them late in summer, eating the petunias. They love the purple flowers. When your hands get close, they spring forward with ease, landing just a few feet away, but well out of reach. Still, the boys have a jar full baking to death in the garage. They insisted that grasshoppers don't need air to breathe. Never punched holes in the top of the aluminum foil the way I was taught. I don't even know for sure if they do need air. Probably doesn't matter much. They never make it to September either way.

Baseball season started late this summer, after the All-Star break. Then we played in the street. First came a chalk home plate, and the next day bases appeared, drawn white squares on the asphalt. I was the Yankees and my son was the Mariners. There were lots of home runs and gleeful chases home. Somehow, the Mariners always scored. The Yankees never got to bat. No time for the old team in summer.

No time for reading either, despite the abundance of good books. Getting through a chapter without interruption was unsettling. As a parent, you learn to equate stillness with danger. Too often, when the voices subside and the small patter of excited feet fades, trouble is near.

The kids are fine, thank God, but my concentration is shot. It's not my turn, I know. I had my summers years ago. Spent them like good money on daydreams and baseball cards, superhero comics, and popsicles in three colors shaped like jets. Or on the beach frying like a piece of bacon before the sun went bad and started causing cancer. Even as a child, I knew they couldn't last, that other seasons would intrude and force their falls and winters into life.

When summer started, I challenged my daughter to read a few books, to keep her edge for the rigors of sixth grade coming up. But she let her edge soften into the summer heat, played with dolls for maybe the last time, sang in her room, and slept in late. When I asked her about the book list, she said summer doesn't last forever. And I knew she was right.

The Swings

I dreamed about the swings last night. They were still standing in the corner of the back yard, my two children swinging happily on a summer day. But the swings came down a few months ago, and are just a memory now.

My daughter is fifteen and my son is eleven, too old now for the swings. When I took the set down to make way for a hot tub slab, I thought about the day, ten years earlier, when I constructed them. I remember feeling glad that they were made of real wood, dripping wet in the pouring rain with my wrenches and bolts, a diagram from the manufacturer held to the ground with my boot. I felt like a good dad that day.

When I was a child, swings were made of round metal poles that fit together like pipe cleaners. They rusted out at the edges and creaked where they needed oil. I thought that real wood was progress, something better for my own children.

But when I was done disassembling the wood swings, the magic in them was gone and they looked like nothing but a stack of wet kindling.

In the dream, I was looking down from an upstairs window. I thought I better get down there and enjoy some carefree time on the swings with my kids. For some reason, the upstairs seemed to represent heaven. Maybe I was there in the dream. You're never sure with dreams, though.

We were on vacation in the Caribbean a few weeks ago. As I look back at the fun adventures we had, it all seems like a dream too. On the trip, I was sitting on the deck of our stateroom on the boat, thinking I can't believe I'm here, looking out at the wide expanse of deep blue, frosted with white windcaps far out onto the horizon. Now, back on dry land, thousands of miles away, the whole voyage seems like another dream.

Maybe we dream our whole lives away, and life is like a waking sleep. One day, we turn around and realize that it's all been an unreal adventure. The different chapters of our lives folding out from someplace we can't touch. Knowing a chapter only after it's done. Realizing significance in the bittersweet endings of things. Impermanence is the thread that binds these dreams, all our lives.

In my dream, I wanted to keep the swings somehow, unhinge the world, and join my children, safe in the cocoon of childhood, carefree on an unending summer's day.

But the swings passed from one dream world to the next, present to past, flowing in the curious river of time. Now I only see them when I sleep.